NEW TESTAMENT THEOLOGY
TODAY

NEW
TESTAMENT
THEOLOGY
TODAY

by

RUDOLF SCHNACKENBURG

Catholic
Theologic

Translated by David Askew

HERDER AND HERDER

1963
HERDER & HERDER NEW YORK
232 Madison Avenue, New York, NY

This book was first published in Bruges, in 1961, by Desclée de Brouwer et Cie, under the title *La Théologie du Nouveau Testament*, Subsidia 1 in the series *Studia Neotestamentica*.

Nihil Obstat: Joannes M. T. Barton, S.T.D., L.S.S. *Censor deputatus*
Imprimatur: E. Morrogh Bernard, *Vic. Gen.*
Westmonasterii, die 14a Decembris, 1962

Library of Congress Catalog Card Number: 63-9559

© Translation, 1963, Geoffrey Chapman Ltd.

Made and Printed in Great Britain by
Charles Birchall & Sons, Liverpool & London

ABBREVIATIONS

Bib	Biblica
BZ	Biblische Zeitschrift
CBQ	The Catholic Biblical Quarterly
DBS	Dictionnaire de la Bible. Supplement.
JBL	The Journal of Biblical Literature.
JTS	Journal of Theological Studies
NT	Novum Testamentum
NTS	New Testament Studies
RB	Revue Biblique
TW	Theologisches Wörterbuch zum Neuen Testament
ZNW	Zeitschrift fur die neutestamentliche Wissenschaft

An italic numeral immediately following the title of a book indicates the edition to which reference is made.

CONTENTS

FOREWORD

When an international team of Catholic biblical scholars agreed with Desclée de Brouwer publishers in 1959 to launch a new series of biblical monographs, *Studia Neo-testamentica,* they could hardly foresee the remarkable success that would come to the first volume which is now presented in English translation. This series is twofold : scientific mongraphs on various aspects of New Testament studies (*Studia*), and works which present the acquired results and the state of research in various branches of New Testament study (*Subsidia*).

The work of Father Schnackenburg was published in the *Subsidia* and it quickly won universal approval. In the *Journal of Biblical Literature* Professor Otto Piper hailed it in the perspective of the ecumenical movement, noting the interest of Roman Catholic theologians in biblical studies. Father Bruce Vawter, C.M., in the *Catholic Biblical Quarterly* stressed the pertinence of our book for the systematic theologian as well as for the biblical student.

Here I would prefer to underline its essential appeal to all Christians who are presumably interested in the historical origins of their faith. A theology of the New Testament is not an assembling of various proof texts, arranged within the framework of a theological system. Rather, it is the presentation of the historical genesis and gradual growth of New Testament doctrines. But Father Schnackenburg does not directly aim at such a presentation; his purpose is to give an overview of the divergent and vital tendencies in the early Church—the grist of a more systematic biblical theology—as these have been captured and analyzed through the efforts of modern research. What has current scholarship discovered concerning the phrase, 'Son of Man'? What is the moral and ascetical tone of New Testament teaching and how does it relate to the concrete Christian life of today? What is the nuance of the Pauline phrase, 'Body of Christ'? These and similar questions have been pursued by New Testament scholars in recent times. The author surveys the present trend in these studies and expresses an informed judgment upon them.

There is hardly a person, Catholic or non-Catholic, who has not become aware of the so-called 'new look' in the current biblical movement, which was inaugurated for Catholics by the 1943 encyclical of Pope Pius XII, *Divino afflante Spiritu*. This was an *aggiornamento* in one particular field which anticipated the call to modernization that was sounded by Pope John XXIII in Vatican Council II. It was to be expected that exaggerations might appear in this challenging study of biblical literary forms, but the gains have far outweighed the losses, which have of their own weight fallen into the limbo of unproved and forgotten theories. With fine clarity and in sharp outline Father Schnackenburg illustrates these gains; he presents the results of recent scholarly investigations dealing with the Synoptic Gospels, the Johannine writings, the Pauline corpus, and the Catholic Epistles. One may single out particularly the progress made in the study of Pauline theology, which if it cannot be systematized, now stands out in all its rich variations, or the new insights into the thought of St John. Especially valuable is the author's sifting and evaluation of a wide range of literature, both Catholic and non-Catholic, e.g., the treatment of Bultmann and of Cullmann's Christological study.

His masterful sweep through the New Testament has enabled Father Schnackenburg to go beyond mere assessment and he points out how much remains to be done. As general works, the New Testament theologies written by Fathers Meinertz and

Bonsirven (neither of them in English translation) are not really adequate. Besides, there are many specialized areas that are calling for more detailed treatment : the State and the New Testament, St John and gnosticism, the meaning of sin in St John, the biblical roots of Christian spirituality, etc. At times he recognizes frankly that there is no adequate Catholic literature on specific topics. This can only be a spur to an already alert group of Catholic scholars who are deeply involved in the vital science of exegesis which is emerging today. And Rudolf Schnackenburg has happily been in the forefront of this advance, with his studies on New Testament morality (1954) and the Kingdom of God (1959). These and many other publications have made his a well-known name in European and American biblical circles. At present he is professor of New Testament exegesis at the University of Würzburg, Germany, and co-editor of the scholarly biblical periodical, *Biblische Zeitschrift*.

ROLAND E. MURPHY, O. CARM.
The Catholic University of America

CHAPTER I

THE GENERAL PROBLEM OF NEW TESTAMENT THEOLOGY

SCIENTIFIC KNOWLEDGE OF THE Bible owes its growing importance largely to the development of New Testament theology.
Work in this new and promising branch of biblical studies has
been recognized as one of the the tasks our age must attempt.[1]
True, Pope Pius XII who, in his encyclical *Divino Afflante
Spiritu*, called upon exegetes to reveal the theological content
of every book and every text in the Bible, did avoid using the
term 'New Testament theology';[2] but this was because, although there is frequent talk about this field of study today,
there is very little real awareness of the problems it raises. And
yet the questions relating to New Testament theology—questions about its legitimacy, its import, its tasks and the way in
which it should be set out—have recently provoked lively discussion among both Catholics and Protestants.[3] We shall turn
our attention to these fundamental questions first of all.

---

[1] Cf. A. BEA, *Der heutige Stand der Bibelwissenschaft*, in *Stimmen der Zeit*,
79, 1953-1954, 91-104, particularly 101.
[2] *Enchiridion Biblicum* 2, Naples-Rome, 1954, No. 551.
[3] Catholics: W. HILLMAN, *Wege zur neutestamentlichen Theologie*, in
Wissenschaft und Weisheit, 14, 1951, 56-67, 200-211; 15, 1952, 15-32,
122-136; F.-M. BRAUN, *La théologie biblique*, in *Revue Thomiste*, 61, 1953,
221-253; M. MEINERTZ, *Sinn und Bedeutung der neutestamentlichen Theologie*,
in *Münchener Theologische Zeitschrift*, 5, 1954, 159-170; V. WARNACH,

I. THE POSSIBILITY AND LEGITIMACY OF A NEW TESTAMENT
THEOLOGY.

Historically speaking, New Testament theology was first
mentioned among Protestants, in the course of the controversy
between the supporters of a 'scholastic' theology and the fol-
lowers of a 'biblico-dogmatic' theology. During the nineteenth
century, New Testament theology became an autonomous field

Gedanken zur neutestamentlichen Theologie, in *Gloria Dei*, 7, 1952, 65-75;
G. SPICQ, *L'avènement de la théologie biblique*, in *Revue des Sciences Philoso-
phiques et Théologiques*, 35, 1951, 561-574; R. SCHNACKENBURG,
Botschaft des Neuen Testamentes, in *Heilige Schrift und Seelsorge*, Vienna,
1955, 110-127; S. LYONNET, *De notione et momento theologiae biblicae*, in
Verbum Domini, 34, 1956, 142-153; H. SCHLIER, *Über Sinn und Aufgabe
einer Theologie des Neuen Testaments*, BZ, 1, 1957, 5-23; W. HILLMANN,
Grundzüge der urchristlichen Glaubensverkündigung, in *Wissenschaft und
Weisheit*, 20, 1957, 163-180; C. SPICQ, *Nouvelles réflexions sur la théologie
biblique*, in *Revue des Sciences Philosophiques et Théologiques*, 42, 1958,
209-219; K. RAHNER, *Biblische Theologie und Dogmatik in ihrem wechsel-
seitigen Verhältnis*, in *Lexikon für Theologie und Kirche 2*, vol. 2, Freiburg in
Br., 1958, 449-451; A. DESCAMPS, *Réflexions sur la méthode en Théologie
Biblique*, in *Sacra Pagina*, 1, Gembloux, 1959, 132-157; M. PEINADOR,
La integración de la Exegesis en la teología, ibid., 158-179; D. M. STANLEY,
Towards a Biblical Theology of the New Testament, The McAnley
Lectures 1958, West Hartford, 1959, 267-281.

Protestants: A. N. WILDER, *New Testament Theology in Transition*, in
Study of the Bible Today and Tomorrow, 1947, 419-436; F. C. GRANT,
An Introduction to New Testament Thought, New York, 1950, 18-28;
BO REICKE, *Einheitlichkeit oder verschiedene 'Lehrbegriffe' in der ntl. Th.?* in
Theologische Zeitschrift, Bâle, 9, 1953, 401-415; E. STAUFFER, *Prinzipien-
fragen der ntl. Th.*, in *Ev. luther. Kirchenzeitung*, 4, 1950, 327-329;
A. J. B. HIGGINS, *The Growth of New Testament Theology*, in *Scottish
Journal of Theology*, 6, 1953, 275-286; G. EBELING, *The Meaning of
'Biblical Theology'*, in *Journal of Theological Studies*, 6, 1955, 210-225;
R. BULTMANN, *Epilegomena*, in *Theologie des Neuen Testaments*, Tubingen,
1953, 577-591, (English translation in 2 vols.); G. H. WOOD, *The
Present Position of New Testament Theology: Retrospect and Prospect*, NTS, 4,
1957-1958, 169-182; A. RICHARDSON, *An Introduction to the Theology of the
New Testament*, London, 1958, 9-15.

of study, distinguished from 'systematic theology' by its aims and methods.[1]

To the Catholic mind, theology—that is, the study of Revelation in the light of reason—is essentially a dogmatic study, which adds tradition to sacred Scripture as a source of faith, and which must always submit to the magisterium of the Church, the immediate rule of faith. But today we can see more clearly that merely to surround articles of faith with 'dicta probantia', and to string together biblical passages in order to construct a dogmatic system, is a practice which does not take full account of the value and originality of sacred Scripture; and, equally, which fails to recognize the basic role which the data of faith play in any theological elaboration.[2] Theology did not have its beginning when Revelation was explained and systematized with the help of Greek philosophy; it was there, already, in the Bible itself. Hebrew thought—which is the predominant type of thought in the Bible—is articulated in a different way from Western, Greek thought;[3] but the theological statements of Scripture are none the less profound or moving because of it. And we can even say that, from many points of view, this Semitic thought is closer to contemporary existentialist thought, and is more readily accessible to those who belong to the existentialist school. [4]

But we cannot classify exegesis among the purely historical sciences, since it goes further than merely explaining the Bible with the help of the methods of philology and comparative

---

[1] Cf. G. EBELING, art. cit., 210-220; H. SCHLIER, in Lexikon für Theologie und Kirche 2, vol. 2, Freiburg in Br., 1958, 444-447.

[2] K. RAHNER, art. cit., 449.

[3] Cf. TH. BOMAN, Das hebräische Denken im Vergleich mit dem griechischen 3, Gottingen, 1959, (English translation 1960); C. TRESMONTANT, Essai sur la pensée hébraïque, Paris, 1953, (German translation: Biblisches Denken und hellenische Überlieferung, Dusseldorf, 1956).

[4] Cf. J. HESSEN, Griechische oder biblische Theologie? Leipzig, 1956.

religion, to recognize that its task is to interpret these disciplines
theologically in the light of faith. Even when New Testament
theology is content simply to array the biblical authors' theological statements in a 'positive' way and to show how they
have been synthesized, while refusing to probe into them in a
speculative way, still it is a genuine theology. Real theological
work is needed for an understanding of the 'original' genre of
these biblical statements and, equally, for their systematic
arrangement.[1] As C. Spicq has very justly pointed out, dogmatic theology and biblical theology differ only in their func-
tions: 'The first seeks to understand Revelation with the help
of rational philosophy, while the second seeks to understand it
in the sacred texts themselves; the first uses primarily meta-
physics and logic, while the second relies on philology and
history.'[2]

Their methods differ, at least in part; but they are one at a
deeper level, for biblical theology, too, is led by the 'sense of
faith' and goes forward κατὰ τὴν ἀναλογίαν τῆς πίστεως
(Rom. 12.6).[3] Hence it is not possible for dogmatic theology
and New Testament theology to be opposed to one another,
either in their content or in their outcome—they simply probe
into, and light up, the same Revelation from two different
standpoints; what is more they are the complement of each
other.

New Testament theology is still a new field, and is still fairly
shapeless and incomplete, but its roots are strong, and the
source from which it springs is fruitful. So we may not call
into question either the possibility or the legitimacy of New

---

[1] Cf. c. spicq, in *Revue des Sciences Phil. et Théol.*, 35, 1951, 563 f.
[2] *Ibid.*, 571.
[3] Cf. R. schnackenburg, *Der Weg der katholischen Exegese*, BZ, 2,
1958, 161-176.

Testament theology, which today is justified in claiming a major role in the general field of theology.[1]

2. REVELATION—THE KERYGMA AND THE CONFESSION OF FAITH—THEOLOGY.

A difficulty for New Testament theology arises from the very originality and historical nature of the New Testament. This document, sacred to our faith, is not primarily an exposition, not even the earliest and most authoritative exposition, of the revelation brought once and for all by Jesus Christ (Heb. 1.1): first and foremost, it is the actual book of the Revelation, and hence the privileged *source* for all Christian theology. But is it possible to distinguish the Revelation of the New Testament from its theological presentation in the New Testament? Can we put our fingers on the exact place where formal revelations have been made, can we show exactly where the theological judgements which interpret them begin? The early Church has not simply handed down the Revelation of Jesus Christ exactly as it was, but has always understood it in the light of the paschal events. This problem is discussed by Protestants as well as Catholics,[2] but a clear-cut solution is still nowhere in sight. The words spoken by Jesus, in which Revelation has been preserved in its purest state, have not simply been written down verbatim in the Synoptics; for the most part, the mere fact that they have been selected, arranged and formulated means that an interpretation has already been put upon them. What is more, Jesus' *acts,* and particularly the saving *events* of the Cross and Resurrection, are just as much a part of Revelation.

[1] Cf. F.-M. BRAUN, *art. cit.,* 233-237; cf. also L. ALONSO-SCHÖKEL, *Argument d'Écriture et théologie biblique dans l'enseignement théologique,* in *Nouvelle Revue Théologique,* 91, 1959, 337-354.
[2] H. SCHLIER, *art. cit.,* 14 f.; G. EBELING, *art. cit.,* 222.

And it simply is not possible to set down these facts outside any context of belief or theology.

So, from the very beginning, we find, mingled with the handing down of Revelation, theological statements which throw light on that Revelation and explain it. We must look on these statements as the very first Christian theology or, better, as the basis for all theology. This first layer has still a primitive and anonymous character about it, for the theologians who were at work do not display any very marked personality.[1] But behind them stand the Apostles in their role as 'witnesses' to, and 'interpreters' of, Christ's revelation, and the early Church responded to their message with confessions of faith, prayers and doxologies.[2] Thus, the 'kerygma' and the 'confession of faith' were the first 'forms' in which faith was expressed and theology took shape. It would be as well to avoid using the expression 'community theology' to designate this, for there is one Protestant critical school which takes the expression to mean the inventions of the post-Pentecostal community, inventions which, at least to some extent, had no foundation in Christ's revelation.[3] We should prefer to use the expression 'theology of the first apostles and of the early Church' to designate those commonly held theological ideas, which were based on the testimony of the Apostles and adopted by the whole body of the early Church.

On the basis of this primitive layer were built up the theological systems of each of the masters and preachers, who used

[1] Cf. J. BONSIRVEN, *Théologie du Nouveau Testament*, Paris, 1951, 25 f.; with others, he speaks of a 'fifth Gospel'.

[2] Cf. C. H. DODD, *The Apostolic Preaching and its Developments*, London, 1944; O. CULLMANN, *Die ersten christlichen Glaubensbekenntnisse 2*, Zollikon-Zurich, 1949.

[3] Cf. F. MUSSNER, Art., *Gemeindetheologie*, in *Lexikon für Theologie und Kirche 2*, vol. 4, Freiburg in Br., 1960, 646-648.

a system of ideas personal to themselves, developed a large number of concepts, and gave their own special structure to the message they preached. (We are here speaking of theologians of the early Church in the full sense of the word theologian : men like Paul and John and the author of the Epistle to the Hebrews.)

Hence we must distinguish the 'theology of the early Church' in its most ancient (apostolic) form, from Jesus' message, which constituted the immediate revelation. Then we must go on to enquire how Revelation, and the theological interpretation of the Old Testament by Jesus and by the Church, were returned to and reworked.

The theological position adopted by Jesus towards the Old Testament and towards Jewish theology acquires the value of revelation because he was who he was (cf. his authoritative standpoint towards the Law); but the early Church's christological interpretation of Scripture was already in the order of theology; and inversely, the earliest Christian theology was, generally speaking, sheer scriptural theology.[1] The task of bringing unity to a theology of the Old and the New Testaments, a theology constructed on the different levels of Revelation and of the history of salvation, is a difficult one, which has hitherto been tackled in only a groping and unsatisfying manner.[2]

---

[1] Cf. L. VENARD, *Citations de l'A.T. dans le N.T.*, DBS II, Paris, 1934, 23-51; J. DUPONT, *L'utilisation apologétique de l'A. T. dans les discours des Actes*, in *Ephemerides Theol. Lovanienses*, 29, 1953, 289-327; C. H. DODD, *According to the Scriptures*, London, 1952; C. SMITS, *Oud-Testamentische citaten in het Nieuwe Testament*, 3 vols., Bois-le-Duc, 1952-1957; R. V. G. TASKER, *The Old Testament in the New Testament 2*, London, 1954.

[2] Cf. P. LESTRINGANT, *Essai sur l'unité de la révélation biblique*, Paris, 1942; M. BURROWS, *An Outline of Biblical Theology*, Philadelphia, 1946; G. E. WRIGHT, *God Who Acts (Studies in Biblical Theology, 8)*, London, 1952; J. GUILLET, *Thèmes Bibliques*, Paris, 1951 (German edition, Lucerne, 1954).

3. THE UNITY AND THE DIVERSITY OF NEW TESTAMENT THEOLOGY.

From the various works of the New Testament—behind which stand particular authors and 'theologians'—we get an impression of a great variety of theological standpoints; in the field of christology, for instance, we can make out a great number of 'theologies'.[1] Can we, then, really talk about a New Testament theology? We can and we must, precisely because the New Testament is a unity, as Protestant exegetes also are insisting.[2] The various works which have been brought together in the New Testament, and which the Church has recognized in her canon, are at one in the confession of *one* Lord, *one* faith, *one* baptism, and *one* God and Father (Eph. 4.5, 6). Only when we listen exclusively to comparative religion and regard the early Church as one of those social groups that spring up under various influences (and the majority of these theories are in any case open to question) is it possible for this 'unity in diversity' to be largely lost to view. If we are to see this unity, we need the perspective of theology. Those who can see that the different witnesses felt themselves bound to a common belief will alone hear from the various voices of the choir the same harmony. The *formal* principle of the unity of New Testament theology is thus the common faith of the early Church; but its *material* unity is more difficult to discover. And it is

[1] Cf. R. P. CASEY, *The Earliest Christologies*, in *Journal of Theological Studies*, 9, 1958, 253-277.

[2] Cf. F. C. GRANT, *op. cit.*, 29-42 (cf. 20: 'Yet one may wonder if the pendulum has not swung too far, and if there is not really a greater unity in Scripture, especially in the New Testament than the atomistic, purely exegetical, purely historical interpretation of "New Testament religion" takes for granted'); Bo REICKE, A. RICHARDSON, *loc. cit.*,; A. M. HUNTER, *The Unity of the New Testament*, London, 1957 (German translation 1959).

still more difficult to decide what *practical* starting-point we should adopt if we wish to express in objective words the unity of New Testament theology.

Several suggestions have been made in this regard—christology,[1] the history of salvation (which would give us a general view of the whole eschatological process of redemption),[2] and charity (which is the basic theme of New Testament theology).[3] The earliest Christian theologians did not themselves follow any systematic plan in their writings, which were, for the most part, occasional works. And they did not bother to compare their own writings with those of the other Apostles.

Because of this, one problem still remains : ought we to keep to the language and ideas proper to each author, or should we attempt to grasp that content of Revelation which is common to them all, and then express it in our own way?[4] To some extent, anyone who writes about New Testament theology can-not help introducing new and more universal concepts which are not to be found formally in the New Testament, but which do express New Testament thought—concepts like 'the history of salvation', 'eschatology', 'sacraments' and 'christocentricism'. But the danger of this is that we might force living forms into clothing which does not suit them (e.g. scholastic terminology) and thus destroy their vitality.

---

[1] Bo REICKE, *art. cit.*, 408-413.

[2] E. STAUFFER, *Die Theologie des Neuen Testaments 4*, Stuttgart, 1948 (English translation 1955); A. M. HUNTER, *Introducing New Testament Theology*, London, 1957.

[3] V. WARNACH, *Agape. Die Liebe als Grundmotiv der ntl. Th.*, Dusseldorf, 1951; cf. C. SPICQ, in *Revue des Sciences Phil. et Théol.* 42, 1958, p. 212 f. and note 16.

[4] C. SPICQ, *art. cit.*, 213.

4. THE PLAN AND STRUCTURE OF A NEW TESTAMENT THEOLOGY.

Since New Testament theology must be related to an historical study of the theological concepts which meet and are developed in the New Testament, it must itself necessarily trace an historical line of development : from the preaching of Christ to the visions of the Apocalypse, from the community in Jerusalem to Hellenistic Christianity, from Paul and the theologians who are related to him to John and the Johannine milieu. But this method of procedure (which has seemed invincible to fervent supporters of 'Religionsgeschichte'[1] such as H. J. Holtzmann, W. Bousset, H. Weinel and others) can be attacked on several grounds;

1. The chronological order is not absolutely certain, and the so-called 'development' is highly disputable.

2. A New Testament theology of this kind seems to be indistinguishable from comparative religion; it does not lay bare the theological tenets of the New Testament, nor does it really demand our assent to them.[2]

3. The unity of New Testament theology is destroyed, since this school is content merely to set out the ideas and the views of each individual thinker or preacher (cf. above pp. 22-3).

This is why a more thematic and systematic presentation is needed. In this context, E. Stauffer has made an original study.[3] He does not trace historical development, but follows the sequence of the events of salvation, and turns for information, on each point of importance, to the witnesses and the testimony that we find throughout the New Testament. This has resulted

---

[1] The history of religion, comparative religion.
[2] Cf. R. BULTMANN, *Epilegomena*, in *Theologie*, 590 f.
[3] See p. 23 n. 2.

in an historical theology of the New Testament which is christ-ocentric in character, but which does little to display the originality of the various theologians, who are here dealt with in the mass. Others, following the path of theme and synthesis, have not tried to say everything, and deal only with a few central themes.[1] The weakness of this sort of theological presen-tation is the lack, or at least the blurring, of historical relief, the destruction of personal characteristics and the levelling of differences, which are yet one of the riches of New Testament theology. Therefore the two great Catholic works of M. Meinertz and J. Bonsirven[2] have in the main kept faithfully to the historical method, with its emphasis on differences, while constantly showing the cohesion of New Testament theology. C. Spicq disagrees with this approach; his preference is for a unified concept, for example, the idea of *Agape,* rather as V. Warnach focuses on the theology of the mysteries.[3] A work in several volumes,[4] which embraces both the Old and the New Testaments and follows the scholastic method of division, con-stitutes less a true biblical theology than a biblical substructure of dogmatic theology.

It seems that an acceptable solution to this issue lies in the synthesis of these two contrasting approaches. In his *New Testament Theology,* which has seen many new editions, P. Feine follows the historical method,[5] but he does at least end by summing up remarkably well 'the key ideas of New Testament

---

[1] F. C. GRANT, A. M. HUNTER, *Introducing,* A. RICHARDSON, *op. cit.,* and others.

[2] M. MEINERTZ, *Theologie des Neuen Testaments,* 2 vols., Bonn 1950; J. BONSIRVEN, *Théologie du Nouveau Testament,* Paris, 1951.

[3] See note 3, p. 23 above.

[4] F. C. CEUPPENS, *Theologia biblica,* I: *De Deo Uno 2,* Turin-Rome, 1949; II: *De Deo Trino 2,* 1949; III: *De Incarnatione,* 1950; IV: *De Mariologia,* 1949.

[5] P. FEINE, *Theologie des Neuen Testaments 8,* Berlin, 1951.

theology'. H. Schlier, too, after presenting the tradition of the community and the theology of the Synoptics and of Paul and John, tries, using several great themes as his foundation—God, the divine government, Jesus Christ, the Holy Ghost, the Church, faith, the new life—to emphasize the inner unity of the various theologies, and to show the hidden foundation and the unseen, unifying link of New Testament theology.[1]

In order to construct this New Testament theology, one question is most important : can the preaching of Jesus himself be taken as a part of this theology, or, since it is an eschatological revelation, must it rather provide the basis, and the assumed data, for any New Testament theology? Meinertz and Bonsirven give the place of first and greatest importance to this preaching. And, indeed, it would not be possible to exclude Jesus' message with its central themes of the kingdom of God, the divine fatherhood, charity etc., from any New Testament theology. But, when we turn to St John's Gospel, the difficulty becomes clear : are we really going to fuse this Gospel with the Synoptics as far as Jesus' message and teaching are concerned (Bonsirven), or are we going to consider it separately from them, and see in it the witness of Johannine theology (Meinertz)?

From a theological point of view, Schlier is right to see in the history of Jesus, not a part of New Testament theology, but its assumed basis (although he does not accept Bultmann's critical position[2]). But this is only a half-truth, for in the Synoptics, and especially, as one would expect, in John, Jesus' life and deeds have as such been made a part of the evangelists' own theology. For this reason it would be closer to the facts of the situation to accept the new consensus of opinion on the origin-

---

[1] Art. cit. 19.

[2] BULTMANN's reasons are the following: 1. The conviction that the historical Jesus and his message are almost completely out of reach; 2. The idea that it is only the kerygma of the community that matters.

ality of the Gospel traditions.[1] In this view, Jesus' message, and his revelation about himself—a revelation which already implied a christology—together with his life, his deeds, and even his childhood, is presented according to the theology of each individual evangelist, who are all, to some extent, handing on Revelation, but who are also, to some extent, interpreting it. Thus Jesus' message takes its place in any New Testament theology, not only as Revelation, but also as a theology. It would be best to begin this exposition with the tradition of the Apostles and the early community; then the theology of the synoptic Gospels, beginning, perhaps, with what they have in common, and following with the ideas which are special to Mark, Luke and Matthew.[2] Only then would one develop the theology of Paul, John and the other New Testament theologians, at the same time indicating everything in them that testifies to their continuity with the earliest tradition and to their agreement with the Church's confessions of faith.

An exposition of this sort has not yet been attempted. There is nothing surprising in this. Enough preparatory work has not yet been done on the theology of the early community (cf. Chap. III below) and of the synoptic Gospels (Chap. IV). Nevertheless, we shall try to give a bird's-eye view of such an exposition.

5. NEW TESTAMENT THEOLOGY AND PROGRESS IN BIBLICAL SCIENCES.

In so far as it is a science which, drawing on all the resources of historical research, attempts to establish the thought of the authors of the New Testament, New Testament theology,

---

[1] Cf. J. HUBY, X. LEON-DUFOUR, *L'Évangile et les Évangiles*, in *Verbum Salutis*, XI, Paris, 1954; R. SCHNACKENBURG, art. *Formgeschichtliche Methode*, in *Lexikon für Theologie und Kirche 2*, vol. 4, Freiburg in Br., 211-213, with a bibliography.

[2] Cf. Chapter IV below. The chronological order of the synoptic Gospels is of little importance in such a theological construction.

much more than dogmatic and speculative theology, is dependent on the development and progress of our historical knowledge and of the exegetical knowledge which springs from it. It is, for instance, a matter of some consequence whether we interpret Paul's thought in the context of his Jewish heritage or of his Hellenistic environment. It is a matter of consequence, too, in the case of St John, whether we admit an influence from Qumran, or the hypothesis of his controversy with contemporary gnostic currents of thought, or, again, a closer link with Palestinian or Hellenistic Judaism etc.[1] But we should be deceiving ourselves and falling back into the old mistakes of the school of comparative religion were we to claim that these alternative interpretations are only of relative importance. It is no doubt true that expositions do vary, not only according to the personal views of the writers, but also according to the state of biblical science. But, since Catholic exegesis by virtue of its link with living tradition, with the magisterium of the Church and with the *sensus fidei*, will always hold fast to certain fundamental statements and deductions, any New Testament theology built on this basis will have a guide line to follow and will possess clearly defined features. New Testament theology may prove a typical example of what historical and systematic theologies are capable of when they unite and seek to inter-act upon each other. Such a New Testament theology must be constantly perfecting a better historical and theological understanding; historical facts must be clearly delineated and at the same time be assumed into a vision of faith and given an immediate relevance to the Christian life.

[1] Cf. Chapter V (Paul) and Chapter VI (John) below.

CHAPTER II

THE PRINCIPAL SCHOOLS AND THE MAJOR WORKS

SINCE FOR ANY NEW Testament theology some preliminary standpoint is necessary, manuals, like more extensive works, will reflect the theological positions of their authors. Similarly, the critical-historical method, and the exegesis which depends on it, leads writers to identical judgements. Hence, the differences of opinion which exist in the field of New Testament theology have their root in the main theological schools of thought of the last few decades.

1. COMPARATIVE RELIGION (RELIGIONSGESCHICHTE)

At the turn of the century, the strongest trend was towards comparative religion or, among conservative protestants, towards biblical positivism. As far as the New Testament theology of the nineteenth century is concerned, H. J. Holtzmann's work in two volumes[1] marks both a summit and a *point d'arrivée*. The author attempts to expose and discuss the concepts of the New Testament (the *Lehrbegriffe*[2] of the New Testament authors), but, at the same time, he wants to portray the

[1] H. J. HOLTZMANN, *Lehrbuch der neutestamentlichen Theologie*, 2 vols., Tubingen, Vol. I, 1897, Vol. II, 1911.
[2] 'Systems of thought'.

29

historical development of early Christianity. Here, we can still feel the influence of the school of F. Ch. Baur, whose Hegelian method of reconstructing history had provided his contemporaries with a guiding principle for the understanding of the beginnings of Christianity. The first volume deals with 'Jesus and primitive Christianity' : with the infancy and childhood of the Christian religion. The second volume deals with 'Paulinism', 'deutero-Paulinism', and 'Johannine theology' : we might call this the age of Christianity's stormy adolescence, and of its maturity. But even in the first volume (Chapter III : the theological problems of primitive Christianity), Holtzmann gives us a glimpse of the first development in Christianity : he traces, side by side with 'primitive Christianity', certain 'evolutionary factors and internal oppositions'; he gives the Apocalypse (although this is a late work), as an example, because he thinks that the dominant note of early Christianity was apocalyptic in character.[1] But only Pauline thought was rich with the potentialities for a great future, and had the capacity to influence history : and it possessed these qualities particularly in its evolved form, which had been influenced by Christian 'alexandrianism'; this form is characterized by Holtzmann as a 'Paulinism which had been smoothed down, with its edges and corners rounded off, popularized and made practicable, and tending towards catholicism'.[2] At one time we used to hear the complaint that Holtzmann was not a consistent historian, and that he had not expanded his New Testament theology into a 'religious history of early Christianity'.[3] This regret, like the general expositions of early

---

[1] *Op. cit.*, I, 539.

[2] *Op. cit.*, I, 569.

[3] Cf. W. WREDE, *Über Aufgabe und Methode der sog. neutestamentlichen Theologie*, Gottingen, 1897; cf. W. G. KÜMMEL, *Das Neue Testament, Geschichte der Erforschung seiner Probleme*, Freiburg in Br. and Munich, 1958, 388-391.

Christianity which were attempted in those days, is revealing of one of the characteristics of the period.[1]

H. Weinel did his best to realize the ideal of a New Testament theology constructed entirely on the pattern of comparative religion. He gave his book the sub-title : 'The Religion of Jesus and of Early Christianity',[2] a phrase that speaks not only of a certain way of looking at history which was typical of the 'Forschung'[3] of the period, but also of a special conception of religion. The summit of religious development is a 'moral religion of redemption' and in Christianity, which constitutes this summit, Weinel pays particular attention to the development of 'mysticism', as the most perfect realization of the desire for redemption. Further, Weinel establishes a network of links with the surrounding world : he admits not only Paul's Jewish heritage, but also the influence of the mystery religions of the Hellenistic world on him, and through him, on early Christianity. In St Paul, the two great religious streams of the Eastern world meet—the moral religion of Christ and the mystery religions, the latter as much in their sacramental form as in their spiritualized, or mystical, form; and it was in this way that Christianity achieved a new shape. The struggle between these two trends, and their reconciliation, is the warp and woof

---

[1] K. WEIZSÄCKER, *Das apostolische Zeitalter der christlichen Kirche 3*, Tubingen, 1902; E. VON DOBSCHÜTZ, *Das apostolische Zeitalter*, Leipzig, 1904; *Probleme des apostolischen Zeitalters*, Tubingen, 1917; P. WERNLE, *Die Anfänge unserer Religion 2*, Tubingen, 1904; O. PFLEIDERER, *Das Urchristentum, seine Schriften und Lehren*, 2 vols., Berlin, 1902; J. WEISS (R. KNOPF), *Das Urchristentum*, Gottingen, 1917 (English translation reprinted 1959); E. MEYER, *Ursprung und Anfänge des Christentums*, 3 vols., Stuttgart, 1921-1923, etc. In the same tradition, also, is M. GOGUEL, *La naissance du Christianisme*, Paris, 1946 (English translation 1953); *L'Église primitive*, Paris, 1947.

[2] H. WEINEL, *Biblische Theologie des Neuen Testaments*, Tubingen, 1st. edition 1911, 4th. 1928.

[3] 'Research'.

of events in the religious history of the West.[1] Here again, we can discern the influence of Hegelian thought—the insistence on 'development' and on 'guiding forces', the conception of the New Testament as a text for comparative religion across which the canon strikes an arbitrary boundary!

The most striking specimen of this 'comparative religion period', however, is probably to be found in another work which, although it is not called a 'New Testament Theology', does in fact tackle this theology—admittedly from a fairly individual point of view. This is W. Bousset's *Kyrios Christos*.[2] Here, the canon of the New Testament is deliberately discarded, as we can see from its sub-title : 'The history of belief in Christ, from the beginnings of Christianity to Irenaeus'. It follows the main trends of Christian development on the central theme of faith in Christ, with constant references to comparative religion based on a very wide range of material which is thus placed at the reader's disposal. It is a work of genius, and yet it is one-sided, and today its weaknesses are obvious in the light of the work done by the whole school of comparative religion :[3] Christianity became what it did thanks to its dealings with the Hellenistic mystery religions, thanks to Hermetic philosophy, to gnosticism and to the other religious phenomena of its environment, not forgetting the myths and legends which it took to itself and assimilated. Christ's novel and original message is only one faint voice in the Judaism of the period; the alarming, revolutionary aspects of Christian belief are dissolved in syncre-

---

[1] *Op. cit.*, 341.

[2] W. BOUSSET, *Kyrios Christos, Geschichte des Christusglaubens von den Anfängen des Christentums bis Irenaeus*, Gottingen, 1st. edition 1913, 4th. 1935 (=2nd. 1921).

[3] Cf. K. PRÜMM, *Der christliche Glaube und die altheidnische Welt*, 2 vols., Leipzig, 1935; ID., *Religionsgeschichtliches Handbuch für den Raum der altchristlichen Umwelt*, Rome, 1954 (=1943); G. KITTELL, *Die Religionsgeschichte und das Urchristentum*, Gutersloh, 1932.

tism; the originality of New Testament revelation gives way to the expression (in the thought categories of one period) of convictions which have been common to mankind from the most distant times.[1]

The principal reaction against this purely historical view came with dialectical theology after the first world war. But even earlier than this, conservative Protestant theologians had refused to subscribe to the comparative approach, turning instead to a positivist, biblical one.[2] The reproach of 'biblicism' which was levelled at them was partly justified : it is in fact true that, in their writings, biblical concepts and biblical statements were not sufficiently related to their historical context but were set up as absolutely valid theological formulas. The descriptive form which their exposition took did not sufficiently clarify the theological problems, and the fundamental problem (which biblical theology poses by the mere fact of being historical) was scarcely ever apparent. They were content simply to describe the various 'forms of teaching' of each group of writings in the New Testament, leaving the reader the task of forming a theological judgement on them and rediscovering the unity behind the various theological conceptions found in the New Testament. Thus, they did not do justice either to the demands of history or to those of theology.

---

[1] Cf. W. Bousset, *op. cit.* 74 f.

[2] B. Weiss, *Lehrbuch der Biblischen Theologie des Neuen Testaments* 7, Stuttgart and Berlin, 1903; W. Beyschlag, *Neutestamentliche Theologie* 2, Halle, 1895; A. Schlatter, *Die Geschichte des Christus* 2, Stuttgart, 1923; *Die Theologie der Apostel* 2, Stuttgart, 1922; Th. Zahn, *Grundriss der ntl. Th.*, Leipzig, 1928.

2. SALVATION-HISTORY (HEILSGESCHICHTE)

The standpoints of biblical positivism and of comparative religion were superseded by two movements in particular. One found in the biblical theme of *salvation history* the guiding principle lacking in the earlier writings, while the other approached New Testament theology from the starting-point of the contemporary problem (*existentialist theology*) in the hope that, in this way, theology would become accessible to contemporary man.

The *heilsgeschichtlich* approach was not entirely new; it had appeared in the nineteenth century in a theologian from Erlangen, J. Chr. K. von Hofmann, whose *Biblical theology of the New Testament* was published posthumously.[1] Hints of it also appear in A. Schlatter's two works—his *History of Christ* and *Theology of the Apostles*—in the sense that he is less interested in the various things that Christ taught than in the internal logic of his deeds and actions (preface), and that he gives his second work this motto: 'Peter's work and that of Christ's other disciples results from what the story of Jesus created.'[2] A basic *heilsgeschichtlich* approach was consistently developed by E. Stauffer in a work which is both a manual and a tool for further work.[3] Both historical, and christocentric, his New Testament theology begins with the creation and the Fall, covers the whole duration of the Law and the promise, and culminates in the christological climax; this climax inaugurates a future in which there is room to consider first of all the still unsatisfied needs of creation and the activity of the Enemy, then the Church's field of action, and finally

[1] J. Chr. K. von HOFMANN, *Biblische Theologie des Neuen Testaments*, revised by W. VOLCK, 1886.—Cf. K. G. STECK, *Die Idee der Heilsgeschichte* (*Theol. Studien* 56), Zurich, 1959.

[2] A. SCHLATTER, *Theologie der Apostel*, 11.

[3] *Op. cit.* (Chapter I, note 2 p. 23 above).

the full revelation of Christ, the restoration of the universe and the final glorification of God. But the most important representative of the theology of salvation-history is O. Cullmann; although he has not written any manual of New Testament theology, he has produced a number of striking works, particularly his pilot book *Christ and Time*.[1] The advocates of 'salvation-history' have been attacked, and many of their opinions are certainly open to question, in particular their way of dividing history into periods, and their excessively rigid systematizations. But we cannot deny that salvation-history is one of the fundamental categories of biblical thought, and does accord with the tension between 'promise' and 'fulfilment' which marks the whole of biblical history from the Fall down to the eschatological consummation.[2]

3. EXISTENTIALIST THEOLOGY

New Testament theology appears in a completely different light in the existentialist theology of R. Bultmann. According to him, its task is to clarify our understanding of self when we are confronted by the kerygma[3]—a formula which cannot be understood except in the general context of his highly contro-

---

[1] O. CULLMANN, *Christus und die Zeit. Die urchristliche Zeit-und Geschichtsauffassung 2*, Zollikon-Zurich, 1948; French edition: *Christ et le Temps, Temps et histoire dans le christianisme primitif*, Paris, 1947; English edition: *Christ and Time*, 1951; cf. *Le retour du Christ (Cahiers théol. de l'actualité prot., 1)*, Neuchâtel-Paris, 1948; *Königsherrschaft Christi und Kirche im Neuen Testament (Theol. Studien, 10)*, Zollikon-Zurich, 1946; *The Early Church* (A. J. B. HIGGINS ed.), London, 1956; cf. also the book by his pupil M. RISSI, *Zeit und Geschichte in der Offenbarung des Johannes (Abhandlungen zur Theologie des Alten und Neuen Testaments, 22)*, Zurich, 1952.

[2] Cf. J. SCHILDENBERGER, *Verheissung und Erfüllung*, Bib, 24, 1943, 107-124, 205-230; H. GROSS, *Zum Problem Verheissung und Erfüllung*, BZ, 3, 1959, 3-17.

[3] R. BULTMANN, *Theologie*, 591.

versial theology.[1] Bultmann starts from our understanding of human existence—an understanding which is renewed by faith in Christ. He looks upon New Testament theology as the explanation of this new understanding of self which the believer has. He does not claim to describe the modes of thought and the symbols of the New Testament as an historian would : what he wishes to do is to study the unfolding of faith itself, on the basis of the new picture of God, the world and man which faith gives. Although this study leans heavily on the historical method its aim is not to reconstruct the past : it is concerned with interpreting the works of the New Testament, in the belief that they contain a message relevant to the present day.[2] According to Bultmann, this contemporary relevance is to be found in the kerygma—in that proclamation of the epic story of Christ which makes modern man face the eschatological decision, forcing him to decide whether or not he wishes to conceive of himself as crucified with Christ and, consequently, as risen with him.[3] There is no need for us to go into the question of the truth of this theology of the kerygma here;[4] but it is at least a remarkable change from the historical and comparative religion problems current at the beginning of the century. This investigator, nurtured in the critical school, puts first emphasis on the theological interest, and draws from the early Church's

---

[1] Among the many works on this subject, we would give a special place to: L. MALEVEZ, *Le message chrétien et le mythe,* Brussels-Bruges-Paris, 1954; R. MARLÉ, *Bultmann et l'interprétation du Nouveau Testament,* Paris, 1956; A. VÖGTLE, *Rivelazione e Mito,* in *Problemi e Orientamenti di Teologia Dommatica,* Milan, 1957, 827-960 (bibliog.); ID., *Rudolf Bultmanns Existenztheologie in Katholischer Sicht,* BZ, 1, 1957, 136-151.

[2] R. BULTMANN, *Theologie,* 591.

[3] R. BULTMANN, *Neues Testament und Mythologie,* in *Kerygma und Mythos,* I, Hamburg, 1948, 15-53, here 51.

[4] Cf. P. ALTHAUS, *Das sogenannte Kerygma und der historische Jesus* (*Beiträge zur Forderung christlicher Theologie* 48), Gutersloh, 1958 (English translation 1959); B. RIGAUX, *L'historicité de Jésus devant l'exégèse récente,* RB, 65, 1958, 481-522 (with bibliography).

glaubende Selbstverständnis[1] that which is still meaningful for contemporary man. And yet Bultmann believes that this task can only be carried out within the framework of a critical exposition, for only in Pauline and Johannine theology has this fresh evaluation of existence, made possible by the faith, been preserved in its pure state : in the other texts, this understanding, cluttered by a number of excrescences (which gave rise to the 'old Catholicism') has disappeared or been obscured.[2] It is easy to say that Bultmann had turned to his own use many of the debatable theories of the old *religionsgeschichtlich* school, and that he often adopts a hyper-critical position. But, because of his theologian's interest in Paul and John, he succeeds in analysing very many theological concepts in a masterly fashion. This is what gives his work a great value, even for those who do not accept his existentialist theology, or even who think that they must regard it as an erroneous interpretation of the primitive kerygma. Henceforth it is no longer possible for us to renounce the conviction that New Testament theology ought to be something more than an historical inventory of the faith and the theological thought of the early Church.

4. SEVERAL ATTEMPTS AT 'THEOLOGIES'.

It remains for us to glance briefly at the other manuals. P. Feine's book, often reprinted,[3] which places a great deal of material at our disposal, and which gives proof of the author's extensive knowledge, lies somewhere between the biblical positivist position and the critical, comparative religion one, although he always maintains the orthodox Protestant viewpoint. F. Büchsel calls his important work a *History of the Word*

---

[1] 'Believing self-understanding'.
[2] Cf. R. BULTMANN, *Theologie*, Part III; and see the review by R. SCHNACKENBURG in *Münchener Theologische Zeitschrift*, 7, 1956, 303-307.
[3] *Op. cit.*, p. 25 n. 5.

of God in the New Testament,[1] and tries to reveal the leading
lines of this history. We might note that he studies 'the word of
Jesus according to John' at the same time as Jesus' preaching.
His aim is to portray the word of God in its various forms, particularly by following the transition from the Gospels to the
epistles. It is a sort of history of Revelation, of the unfolding of
the word of God through the preaching of men. F. C. Grant's
'Introduction to the Thought of the New Testament',[2] sets out
some basic considerations, describes various aspects of the
mental environment, and systematically examines the whole of
the New Testament with reference to the Old Testament and
to the history of thought right up to the mentality of today (see
the section which deals with miracles). M. Burrows had already
followed this course in his *Outline*,[3] with the difference that he
included the Old Testament as a matter of principle so that he
could confront modern man with the whole of the Bible, seen
as the revelation of the divine will in history. The English
writer, A. Richardson, also follows this thematic method, but
limits himself to the New Testament.[4] He has the art of leading
us into biblical thought itself, in a series of instructive chapters :
'Belief and understanding', 'Knowledge and revelation', 'The
salvific power of God', 'The whole Christ' (the new man, the
new Adam, 'in Christ' etc.), 'The Israel of God'. For the
theologian, this is a most stimulating work.

Finally we must note an attempt of a completely new kind
—the several volumes of M. Albertz' work.[5] The author has

---

[1] F. Büchsel, *Theologie des Neuen Testaments, Geschichte des Wortes
Gottes im NT*, Gutersloh, 1937.

[2] *Op. cit.*, p. 15 n. 3.

[3] *Op. cit.*, p. 21 n. 2.

[4] *Op. cit.*, p. 15 n. 3.

[5] M. Albertz, *Die Botschaft des Neuen Testamentes*, Vol. I : *Die
Entstehung der Botschaft*, 1. *Die Entstehung des Evangeliums*, Zollikon-
Zurich, 1947; 2. *Die Entstehung des Apostolischen Schriftenkanons*, Zollikon-
Zurich, 1952; Vol. II : *Die Entfaltung der Botschaft*: 1. *Die Voraussetzungen*

attempted a thorough reworking of the scope and methods of presentation of the two classic fields of study—'Introduction', and 'Theology'. His introduction in a manner very reminiscent of Form-criticism, is presented as a 'genesis of the Message'. Next, organically dependent on this first exposition, comes the study of 'the unfolding of the Message'. In this second part, the only one to interest us here, after criticizing the way in which all biblical theology has been practised since the 'Aufklärung' (II, 1, 15-21), Albertz leaves the beaten track and describes the content of the message, following 2 Cor. 13.13, under the following headings : 'The grace of the Lord Jesus Christ', 'The love of God' and 'The fellowship of the Holy Spirit'. The sequence and arrangement of the various sections and the choice and presentation of the themes are highly personal, and mirror a special view of faith; for this reason, this original work, which has many key ideas worthy of consideration, can hardly count on any extensive following.[1]

On the Catholic side, we shall note first of all A. Lemonnyer,[2] who, on a limited scale, presents the essential data of New Testament theology in an essentially thematic way (the Kingdom of God and its founder, the new economy of salvation, the Person of Christ); this outline has found a wide audience. In Germany, O. Kuss' introduction[3] had a stimulating effect; it is a guide which aims at giving the reader of the Bible a general outline which will familiarize him with the spiritual world of the New Testament. It is easy to understand why works of this standard should have whetted the appetite and created the

der Botschaft. Der Inhalt der Botschaft, Zollikon-Zurich, 1954; 2. Der Inhalt der Botschaft, Zollikon-Zurich, 1957.

[1] Cf. E. FASCHER, Eine Neuordnung der neutestamentlichen Fachdisziplin? in Theol. Literaturzeitung, 83, 1958, 609-618.

[2] A. LEMONNYER, Théologie du Nouveau Testament, Paris, 1928.

[3] O. KUSS, Die Theologie des Neuen Testaments; Eine Einführung, Regensburg, 1937; French translation: Doctrine du Nouveau Testament à la portée de tous. An adaptation by L. MULLER, Paris, 1938.

desire for more extensive works. These, however, are far from plentiful. M. Meinertz and J. Bonsirven (see Chapter I, section 4, p. 25 above) have set out to reveal the theological ideas of the New Testament in their historical development. In the section dealing with Christ, Meinertz begins with John the Precursor, devotes his central section to Jesus' preaching on the Kingdom of God, and then, under the heading 'The Messenger of the Kingdom of God', deals with the christological questions: 'The man Jesus, Jesus as the Messiah, the Divine Redeemer, the Son of God, the Virgin Birth, and the Resurrection and Ascension'. Bonsirven, who had already devoted a special study to the progressive development of Jesus' teaching,[1] opens his 'Theology' with a christology (the only Son of God), and then sets out Christ's preaching, which again is centred on the theme of the Kingdom of God.[2] For the rest, the order he follows is chronological as far as possible, as it was with Meinertz. The theology of St Paul is the only one which he develops expressly: the other theological data of the New Testament are summarized under the heading 'Christian Maturity'. Both authors make a serious attempt to reveal the permanent and normative character of New Testament theology. But neither of them has managed to eliminate the tension between historical exposition and systematic presentation, between pure description and interpretation. Hence the danger arises that all the problems may not be made sufficiently clear. While we welcome their work with gratitude, we cannot help hoping for fresh research, which will profit from the results of the most recent discussions, to be done.

---

[1] J. BONSIRVEN, *Les enseignements de Jésus-Christ*, Paris, 1946.
[2] Cf. also his book: *Le Règne de Dieu*, Paris, 1957.

5. BIBLICAL DICTIONARIES

In addition to the manuals, we must consider other works for the theology of the whole of the New Testament. First among these are the theological dictionaries. The best known is the indispensable 'Theological Dictionary of the New Testament', which was edited first by G. Kittel, and then by G. Friedrich; it now runs into six volumes (letter ρ), and is still expanding, because the articles are taking on the scope and extent of monographs.[1] As in the more modest work of H. Cremer and J. Kögel[2] the method followed is that of thematic and semantic study; each important expression is studied philologically in non-biblical Greek, in the Old Testament, in Palestinian Judaism and in Hellenistic Judaism and, finally, in the New Testament. This German Protestant work embraces all the available linguistic material, which the authors study in conjunction with a team of philologians, adding synthesis to analysis, and even extending it to theological interpretation, although they always stick to the viewpoint of Protestant orthodoxy and their own personal theological positions. No other work can rival this systematic presentation of all the theological material in the Bible. We can nonetheless congratulate ourselves on the fact that the supplement to the Dictionnaire de la Bible does also contain studies on several important theological expressions which are, of their kind, models of Catholic presentation of the theological themes of the Bible. We may quote the excellent

[1] Theologisches Wörterbuch zum Neuen Testament, edited by G. KITTEL, and, from Vol. V., by G. FRIEDRICH, Stuttgart, 1933-1960; six volumes have been published so far.

[2] H. CREMER (-J. KÖGEL), Biblisch-theologisches Wörterbuch der Neutestamentlichen Graecität, Stuttgart-Gotha, 1st. ed. 1867, 11th. 1923, (English translation reprinted, 1955).

articles on Baptism (I, 852-924, by J. Coppens), the Church
(II, 487-691, by A. Médebielle), Expiation (III, 1-262, by the
same author), Faith (III, 276-310, by P. Antoine), Grace (III,
701-1319, by P. Bonnetain), Judgement (in the Old Testament,
IV, 1321-1344, by R. Pautrel; in the New Testament, 1344-
1394, by D. Mollat), Justice and Justification (IV, 1417-1510,
by L. Cerfaux and A. Descamps), Kenosis (V, 7-161, by
P. Henry) and Kyrios (V, 200-234, by L. Cerfaux). As in the
TW, it has also happened that particularly important themes
are entrusted to several collaborators—themes like Mediation
(V, 983-1394—four authors), the history of which is retraced
from the sumero-accadian religion to the New Testament, Logos
(V, 425-497—five collaborators) and Mysteries (VI, 1-225,—
R. Follet and K. Prümm). The *Lexikon für Theologie und
Kirche,* which since 1957 has again been published by
Herder Verlag (Freiburg in Br.), studies a number of the
expressions of biblical theology; because of their concise
form, and the extensive bibliographical information they give,
these studies form at least a basis for Catholic work in this
field.

In addition to these great scientific works, there is no lack
of biblical dictionaries whose aim is to open the theological
treasures of the New Testament to a wider public. Some, like
E. Kalt's dictionary,[1] and the recent Italian dictionary of F.
Spadafora,[2] are in the tradition of the *Reallexika.* Others, like
J. B. Bauer's *Bibeltheologisches Wörterbuch,*[3] or J. Bonsirven's
Vocabulaire Biblique,[4] are of a more original, and decidedly
theological, stamp. The two approaches meet in A. van den

---

[1] E. KALT, *Biblisches Reallexikon,* 2 vols. Paderborn, 1937-1938.

[2] F. SPADAFORA, *Dizionario Biblico,* Rome, 1955.

[3] *Bibeltheologisches Wörterbuch,* edited by J. B. BAUER, Graz-Vienna-
Cologne, 1959.

[4] J. BONSIRVEN, *Vocabulaire Biblique,* Paris, 1958.

Born's *Bijbels Woordenboek*,[1] and in H. Haag's *Bibellexikon*, which is a revision of van den Born's work for the German speaking public.[2] Equivalent Protestant works which we ought to mention are: R. Luther's *Ntl. Wörterbuch*,[3] E. Osterloh-A. Engelland's *Biblisch-theologiches Handwörterbuch zur Lutherbibel und neueren ubersetzungen*,[4] and J. J. von Allmen's *Vocabulaire Biblique*.[5]

6. MONOGRAPHS AND COMMENTARIES

There are also found valuable contributions published as monographs. Here we shall only mention those which deal with the whole of the New Testament (special studies are dealt with in Chapter VIII below). Extended monographs, dealing with important biblical themes, deserve a favourable welcome, for they throw light on the progress of revelation, on theological differences, and on the development of preaching. On *Agape*—which is the central idea of the Christian religion—there are two great Catholic monographs. V. Warnach's work[6] presents the mystery of salvation from the standpoint of *Agape;* the work stands out for the unity of its conception, the breadth of its enquiry, and the phenomenological, instead of merely philological and historical, method of its procedure. C. Spicq's

---

[1] *Bijbels Woordenboek* 2, edited by A. VAN DEN BORN, Roermond 1954; French translation: *Encyclopédie biblique*, Louvain, 1960.

[2] *Bibellexikon*, edited by H. HAAG, Einsiedeln-Zurich-Cologne, 1951-1956.

[3] R. LUTHER, *Neutestamentliches Wörterbuch 13*, Heidelberg, 1951.

[4] V. OSTERLOH-H. ENGELLAND, *Biblisch-theologisches Handwörterbuch zur Lutherbibel und neueren Übersetzungen*, Gottingen, 1954.

[5] J. J. VON ALLMEN, *Vocabulaire Biblique*, Neuchâtel-Paris, 1954, (English translation 1958).

[6] *Op. cit.* (p. 15 n. 3).

work[1]—three volumes of which have appeared, while a fourth is in preparation—is an analysis of the entire body of the texts. Although the author does give a summary for the various books of the New Testament at the end of his careful exegesis of the principal passages, we should like to see this imposing work crowned by a work of synthesis.[2] It is a regrettable fact that we are still without a study of this sort on faith.[3] Equally surprising is the absence of monographs on the idea of God in the New Testament, apart from one study on the concept of the Kingdom of God in both Testaments.[4] The problem of redemption has often attracted attention,[5] but the problems of prayer and worship much less frequently.[6] We find several different methods of procedure illustrated by the following authors: E. Pax, *Epiphaneia*,[7] adopts the approach of the comparative religion school; L. R. Stachowiak, *Chrestotes*,[8]

[1] C. Spicq, *Agapè. Prolégomènes à une étude de théologie néo-testamentaire.* (*Studia Hellenistica*, 10), Louvain, 1955; *Agapè dans le Nouveau Testament. Analyses des Textes*, 3 vols., Paris, 1958-1959.

[2] Cf. the review by P. Benoit, in RB, 66, 1959, 262-265.

[3] But see the article by P. Antoine, in DBS, III, 276-310; R. Schnackenburg, art. *Glaube*, in *Lexikon für Theologie und Kirche 2*, vol. 4, Freiburg in Br., 913-917; J. Duplacy, *D'où vient l'importance centrale de la foi dans le N.T.?* in *Sacra Pagina*, II, Gembloux, 1959, 430-439. On the Protestant side, cf. particularly A. Schlatter, *Der Glaube im Neuen Testament 4*, Stuttgart, 1927; A. Weiser-R. Bultmann, art. πιστεύω, in TW, VI, 174-230 (bibliography).

[4] R. Schnackenburg, *Gottes Herrschaft und Reich*, Freiburg in Br., 1959 (bibliography).

[5] K. H. Schelkle, *Die Passion Jesus in der Verkündigung des Neuen Testaments*, Heidelberg, 1949; A. Kirchgässner, *Erlösung und Sünde im Neuen Testament*, Freiburg in Br., 1950; S. Lyonnet, *De peccato et redemptione*, I, Rome, 1958.

[6] J. M. Nielen, *Gebet und Gottesdienst im Neuen Testament*, Freiburg in Br., 1937; A. Hamman, *La prière, I: Le Nouveau Testament*, Paris-Tournai, 1959. On the Protestant side, cf. G. Delling, *Der Gottesdienst im Neuen Testament*, Gottingen, 1952 (bibliography).

[7] E. Pax, *Epiphaneia. Ein religionsgeschichtlicher Beitrag zur biblischen Theologie* (*Münchener Theologische Studien*, I, 10), Munich, 1955.

[8] L. R. Stachowiak, *Chrestotes, ihre biblisch-theologische Entwicklung und Eigenart, Studia Friburgensia*, 17, Fribourg (Switzerland), 1957.

follows the biblical development, and F. X. Durrwell, *The Resurrection*,[1] proceeds in a systematic fashion.

But there are important concepts, involving the whole of the New Testament, which still await a Catholic study that will take account of the most recent research, while Protestants have already published many remarkable works in this field:[2] for example, the themes of conversion (μετάνοια), peace, hope, man (the anthropology of the New Testament), suffering, death, the world and even the word of God[3] and the Holy Spirit. It may be interesting to publish collective works, in which several authors deal with the same theme, and throw light on it from different sides: this is what happens in *Recherches Bibliques*[4] (which owe their origin to the Biblical Weeks in Louvain), and in the special numbers of *Lumière et Vie*.[5]

[1] F. X. DURRWELL, *La Résurrection de Jésus, mystère de salut 2*, Paris, 1960; English translation: *The Resurrection*, 1960.

[2] Cf. for example: F. BÜCHSEL, *Der Geist Gottes im Neuen Testament*, Gutersloh, 1926 (with reservations); R. ASTING, *Die Heiligkeit im Urchristentum*, Gottingen, 1930; Id., *Die Verkündigung des Wortes im Urchristentum*, Stuttgart, 1939; G. STÄHLIN, *Skandalon*, Gutersloh, 1930; J. SCHNEIDER, *Doxa*, Gutersloh, 1932; H. Kittel, *Die Herrlichkeit Gottes*, Giessen, 1934; E. G. GULIN, *Die Freude im Neuen Testament*, 2 vols., Helsinki, 1932-1936; N. A. DAHL, *Das Volk Gottes*, Oslo, 1941; W. ELTESTER, *Eikon im Neuen Testament*, Berlin, 1958. Monographs are popular, too, in English; cf. for example the works of C. RYDER SMITH, *The Bible Doctrine of Salvation* (1947), *Man* (1951), *Sin* (1953), *Grace* (1956); H. H. ROWLEY, *The Bible Doctrine of Election*, London, 1950.

[3] Cf. H. SCHLIER, *Wort Gottes; Eine neutestamentliche Besinnung*, in *Rothenfelser Reihe* 4, Wurzburg, 1958; in French: *La notion paulinienne de la Parole de Dieu*, in *Littérature et théologie pauliniennes* (*Rech. bibl.*, V), Louvain, 1960, 127-141.

[4] *Recherches Bibliques*, published under the patronage of the Colloquium Biblicum Lovaniense. I: *L'attente du Messie*, 154; II: *La formation des Évangiles*, 1957; III: *L'Évangile de Jean*, 1958; IV: *La secte de Qumrân et les origines du christianisme*, 1959; V: *Littérature et théologie pauliniennes*, 1960.

[5] *Lumière et Vie, Revue de Formation Doctrinale chrétienne*, Saint-Alban-Leysse (Savoie).—There are many numbers dedicated to purely biblical topics, for example on *Jesus the Son of God* (No. 9), *baptism in the N.T.* (Nos. 26-27), *the Redeemer* (Nos. 15 and 36), *work* (No. 20), *miracles* (No. 33), *the Eucharist* (No. 31), *hope* (No. 41).

The commentators themselves are concentrating increasingly on the theological aspects of the Bible, and are doing this fairly often in specialized 'excursus'. This change can be seen in the growing importance given to New Testament theology by the great commentators of *Études bibliques*.[1] What is more, as we can see in the *Verbum Salutis* series or in Herder's *Theologischer Kommentar,* which unhappily still has not made much headway, exegesis itself is becoming more theological.[2] Even introductory works are beginning to include New Testament theology, as we see in the work which has recently appeared under the direction of A. Feuillet.[3]

Finally, there are several series which are useful for the study of New Testament theology : on the Catholic side, we have *Lectio divina* (published by du Cerf) as well as others aimed at a wider public.[4] On the Protestant side there are *Abhandlungen zur Theologie des Alten und Neuen Bundes,*[5] *Studies in Biblical Theology,*[6] *Cahiers théologiques de l'actualité protestante,*[7] and others. This is the briefest outline of the important activity which abounds today in the field of biblical theology.

---

[1] In the introductions to his commentaries, M.-J. LAGRANGE does not give many pages to the 'doctrinal witness'; C. SPICQ, in his *Hébreux I,* gives more than 60 pages to the subject; B. RIGAUX, in his *Thessaloniciens,* gives about 130.

[2] There is still only R. SCHNACKENBURG, *Die Johannesbriefe,* Freiburg in Br., 1953; cf. also the commentaries by H. SCHLIER on the Epistle to the Galatians (H. A. W. MEYER VII, 10), Gottingen, 1949; on Ephesians, Dusseldorf, 1957; O. KUSS, *Der Römerbrief,* Regensburg, 1st. fasc. 1957, 2nd. fasc. 1959.

[3] *Introduction à la Bible,* under the direction of A. ROBERT and A. FEUILLET, vol. II: *Nouveau Testament,* Tournai, 1959.

[4] *Témoins de Dieu* (éd. du Cerf); in German there are, for example, *Leben aus dem Wort* (Herder, Frieburg in Br.); *Die Botschaft Gottes* (St. Benno-Verlag, Leipzig); *Die Welt der Bibel* (Patmos-Verlag, Dusseldorf).

[5] Edited by W. EICHRODT and O. CULLMANN, Zwingli Verlag, Zurich.

[6] S.C.M. Press, London.

[7] Edited by J. J. VON ALLMEN and J. L. LEUBA, Neuchâtel-Paris.

CHAPTER III

THE KERYGMA AND THE THEOLOGY OF THE EARLY CHURCH

THE THEOLOGY OF THE early Church has always had its place in manuals of New Testament theology—although it has tended to be squeezed in between the exposition of Jesus' preaching on the one hand and of Paul's theology on the other. The primitive character of the theology of the early Church was recognized, but not the fact that it actually constituted the very earliest New Testament theology. J. Gewiess[1] has written a very conscientious, matter-of-fact account of it, tackling all the important theological questions. He shows very clearly the characteristics of the Judeo-Palestinian thought of the first community, strongly orientated towards the Old Testament. But the key position held by the first apostles' message of salvation could not be clearly recognized except through an approach along the lines of *Form- und Traditiongeschichte*. This approach was made ten years later by J. Schmitt.[2] Schmitt, a professor from Strasbourg, focused on one limited, but central, theme —the proclamation by the apostles that Jesus had risen. From this ground, he tackled the general problem of apostolic

---

[1] J. GEWIESS, *Die urapostolische Heilsverkündigung nach der Apostel geschichte*, Breslau, 1939.

[2] J. SCHMITT, *Jésus ressuscité dans la prédication apostolique*, Paris, 1949 (with bibliography).

witness,[1] examining it in its historic and doctrinal expression. He revealed the near interdependence of history and faith, and saw that this really was the 'witness' of men chosen and sent by Jesus himself. He saw also that their authoritative explanation of the events of salvation constitutes the fundamental data for any future theology, since it has created an indefeasible tradition. In his study of the sources, he considered, first, the discourses in the first part of Acts—which he calls 'catechetical summaries'—then the apostolic tradition contained in 1 Cor. 15.3b-5, and finally the baptismal confessions and the traces of ancient prayers (hymns).

Other scholars had already admitted that these texts preserve the apostolic kerygma in its earliest form. In this connection we should mention C. H. Dodd's short, but extremely instructive book on the apostolic preaching.[2] Dodd studied the typical structure of the missionary discourses in Acts; he discovered the same kerygma in the construction of the Synoptics (particularly Mark), and found it once again in John and Paul. The baptismal formulas and the liturgical passages, considered as the basis for the first confessions of faith (without prejudging the issue of what influence was exerted by exorcisms, persecutions and the controversy against false doctors) were studied particularly by O. Cullmann[3]—although he was following in

---

[1] Cf. L. CERFAUX, *Témoins du Christ d'après le livre des Actes*, edited L. CERFAUX, II, Gembloux, 1954, 157-174; H. STRATHMANN, Art. μάρτυς in TW, IV, 477-514; H. TRAUB, *Botschaft und Geschichte. Beiträge zur Frage des Zeugen und der Zeugen*, (*Theol. Studien*, 41), Zollikon-Zurich, 1954; E. GUNTHER, *Zeuge und Märtyrer*, ZNW, 47, 1956, 145-161; N. BROX, Μάρτυς *im Neuen Testament* (an unpublished dissertation work), Munich, 1959.

[2] *Op. cit.*, p. 20 n. 2

[3] *Op. cit.*, p. 20 n. 2

the footsteps of several forerunners.[1] To J. V. Schmitt goes the merit of returning to the idea of an apostolic preaching which bore the future within itself (although he did not distinguish sufficiently between missionary kerygma and community didache) and of divorcing this from the negative conclusions of 'Form-criticism' (which held that the christological message was created on the basis of the paschal faith). It is, in fact, true, as he shows in the last part of his book, that the christology implicit in the paschal kerygma (Jesus is 'Christ', 'Lord' and 'Son of God') is not so much the final reach of the progressively developing primitive faith, as the product of a twin revelation —of Gospel history and paschal fact (176).[2] This does not exclude the possibility that christology continued to be thought about and elaborated : thus, Paul conceives of the risen Christ as a second Adam and as a life-giving Spirit (1 Cor. 15.45). The final stages of this development have been retraced by F. X. Durrwell in chapter II of the book already cited.

The apostle's message of salvation, linked historically by the fact of Jesus' resurrection, also sets in the context of the resurrection all that Jesus did in his lifetime, and interprets the whole of his mission of salvation in the light of the prophecies of the Old Testament and of his own revelation; this literally 'fundamental' import of the primitive message is well brought out by J. R. Geiselmann, a dogmatic theologian from

---

[1] Cf. A. SEEBERG, *Der Katechismus der Urchristenheit*, Leipzig, 1903; H. LIETZMANN, *Die Anfänge des Glaubensbekenntnisses*, in *Festgabe für A. v. Harnack*, Tubingen, 1921, 226-242; P. FEINE, *Die Gestalt des Apostolischen Glaubensbekenntnisses in der Zeit des Neuen Testamentes*, Leipzig, 1925; E. STAUFFER, *Theologie*, 212-216; 322. See also J. N. D. KELLY, *Early Christian Creeds* 2, London, 1960, 6-29.

[2] On the Protestant side, cf. K. H. RENGSTORF, *Die Auferstehung Jesu* 4, Witten Ruhr, 1960; H. GRASS, *Ostergeschehen und Osterberichte*, Gottingen, 1956; G. KOCH, *Die Auferstehung Jesu Christi*, Tubingen, 1959

Tubingen, also.[1] The events of salvation inevitably gave rise to the various forms of apostolic preaching—the witness of the Twelve, the differently articulated witness of St Paul, and finally the *paradosis* of the apostles on Jesus as the Messiah. It is particularly fortunate that Geiselmann regards the oldest form of apostolic preaching as the norm for our own preaching and theology on Jesus. He writes:

> Whoever considers that this way of proclaiming Jesus as the Messiah has only a relative value, conditioned by time and place, and valid only for the Judeo-Palestinian region which first heard it . . . whoever concludes that this preaching of Jesus as the Messiah (he in whom the messianic expectations of the Old Testament were fulfilled and became historical reality) being a theology specifically Judeo-Christian, must inevitably, in other times and places, yield to other forms of the message, simply has not grasped the significance of the kerygma of the first apostles . . . Rather, what we must do is to grasp the reality which lies behind temporal conditioning and relative formulas, and then it becomes clear that this form of preaching is rooted in the history of salvation, that is, in reality, and that any other conclusion can only be vain . . . Henceforward, then, this form of expressing the message constitutes the norm for every proclamation of Jesus as Christ.[2]

As far as the content of the book is concerned, Geiselmann refers to the witness of the first apostles as a christological kerygma: this embraces the whole of Jesus' messianic activities from his baptism in the Jordan to his death, his death itself, his resurrection, ascension and glorification, and his second coming. Hence, the apostles were very much concerned with

[1] J. R. GEISELMANN, *Jesus der Christus, Die Urform des apostolischen Kerygmas als Norm unserer Verkündigung und Theologie von Jesus Christus*, Stuttgart, 1951.

[2] *Op. cit.*, 25.

the Jesus of history, who, at the same time, has now become the Lord of glory. In this context, also, we must view the titles which the early Church gave to Jesus—titles which thus normally have reference to the history of salvation. That Paul himself depended on this primitive preaching is quite clear from the fact that he makes his own its christological formulas and hymns (Phil. 1.6-11).

By this route, Catholic theology is returning to its biblical foundations, and to the *heilsgeschichtlich* way of thinking—which is what we find in the Bible. However, there are still a great many subjects in which a vast field of work lies ready for collaboration between exegetes and dogmatic theologians : for example, the basic questions of witness and of justification by faith, of tradition as the transmission of this witness and of the deposit of faith, of the kerygma in its primitive and its modern forms, as it is conditional upon its historical setting and in its permanent significance.

The dialogue on the principle of tradition has been reopened. Among Protestants, O. Cullmann[1] lends his support to the principle, but insists on drawing a distinction between apostolic and ecclesiastical tradition. Among Catholics, J. Geiselmann suggests a new way of looking at the relationship between Scripture and Tradition.[2]

[1] O. CULLMANN, *Die Tradition als exegetisches, historisches und theologisches Problem*, Zurich, 1954.

[2] J. R. GEISELMANN, *Das Konzil von Trient über das Verhältnis der Heiligen Schrift und der nicht geschriebenen Traditionen*, in *Die mündliche Überlieferung*, edited by M. SCHMAUS, Munich, 1957, 123-206; ID., *Die Tradition*, in *Fragen der Theologie heute*, Einsiedeln-Zurich-Cologne, 1957, 69-108.—See the criticism by H. LENNERZ, *Scriptura sola?*, in *Gregorianum*, 40, 1959, 38-53; cf. also H. HOLSTEIN, *La tradition d'après le Concile de Trente*, in *Recherches de Science Religieuse*, 47, 1959, 367-390. See also (from a Protestant standpoint) E. NIELSEN, *Oral Tradition*, London, 1954; G. GLOEGE, *Offenbarung und Überlieferung*, Hamburg, 1954; J. L. LEUBA, *Der Zusammenhang zwischen Geist und Tradition nach dem Neuen Testament*, in *Kerygma und Dogma*, 4, 1958, 234-250.

R. Bultmann's[1] existentialist conception of the kerygma, the relationship between the Jesus of history and the Christ of faith,[2] the soundness of the apostolic witness and the legitimacy of an 'interpretation' of Jesus' message are all questions intimately bound up with the way we look at and judge this very early layer of the preaching and theology of the apostles and of the early Church.

The problem most immediately affected is that of New Testament christology, which at the moment is reaping the benefit of renewed interest. We shall go into this in more detail later (Chapter VIII), but here we may note that extensive Catholic works on subjects as important as the 'Son of Man' and the 'Son of God' are still lacking, in spite of preparatory works which deserve attention.[3] Admittedly it is difficult to

---

[1] Cf. Chapter II, p. 35 n. 3; in addition, see J. M. DE JONG, *Kerygma. Een Onderzoek naar de Vooronderstellingen van de Theologie van R. Bultmann*, Assen, 1958; G. VAUGHAN JONES, *Christology and Myth in the New Testament*, London, 1956.

[2] Cf. the study by B. RIGAUX, in one of the volumes to appear in *Studia Neotestamentica*. (See above, p. xii.)

[3] From the very extensive literature on the 'Son of Man', we shall pick out especially E. SJÖBERG, *Der Menschensohn im äthiopischen Henochbuch*, Lund, 1946; ID., *Der verborgene Menschensohn in den Evangelien*, Lund, 1955; J. COPPENS, *Le messianisme sapiential et les origines littéraires du Fils de l'homme daniélique, Wisdom in Israel and in the Ancient Near East*, in *Vetus Testamentum*, 3, suppl., presented to H. H. ROWLEY, Leyde, 1955, 33-41; S. MOWINCKEL, *He That Cometh*, Oxford, 1956, 346-450; O. CULLMANN, *Die Christologie des Neuen Testaments*, Tubingen, 1957, 138-198 (English translation 1959); A. J. B. HIGGINS, *Son of Man—Forschung*, in *New Testament Essays, Studies in Memory of T. W. Manson*, Manchester, 1959, 119-135 (bibliog.); H. E. TÖDT, *Der Menschensohn in der synoptischen Überlieferung*, Gutersloh, 1959; E. SCHWEIZER, *Der Menschensohn*, ZNW, 50, 1959, 185-209.

On the 'Son of God' cf. J. BIENECK, *Sohn Gottes als Christusbezeichnung der Synoptiker (Abhandlungen zur Theologie des Alten und Neuen Testaments, 21)*, Zurich, 1951; J. JEREMIAS, Art. παῖς θεοῦ, in TW, V, 676-713; W. GRUNDMANN, *Sohn Gottes*, ZNW, 47, 1956, 113-133; J. JOCZ, *The 'Son of God'*, in *Judaica*, 13, 1957, 129-142; O. CULLMANN, *Christologie* 276-313.

fix the limits of the earliest layer of theology common to the early Church but, were we to gather together everything in the New Testament concerning baptism, and baptismal instructions, confessions and paraneses,[1] we should see that it reaches far beyond the confines of Acts. A wealth of matter could also be found in what is left of the liturgical formulas, ranging from those traces which we find in the epistles to the acclamations and hymns of the Apocalypse.[2] The missionary preaching of the early Church is to be found not only in the discourses of Acts, but also in Paul and perhaps even John. Finally, we must look for teaching on the Church not only in Paul (cf. Chapter V): if we are to discover the early Church's consciousness of herself we must turn also to the other New Testament writings; having done so we shall better be able to understand and justify the Gospel of St Matthew, which is the one most aware of the fact of the Church. We should also pay special attention to the 'prophets' of the early Church, who are increasingly recognized as having had a creative role in the formation of New Testament literature.[3] All this makes us see how important it is to examine in more detail this first layer of the theology of the early Church, seeing it in relation to Jesus' first-hand revelation, and contrasting it with the kerygma of the later hellenistic communities and with the individual theology of certain of the New Testament personalities.

---

[1] On this question, cf. Chapters V, VI, and VII, section 3.

[2] Cf. Chapter VII, section 4, below.

[3] Cf. E. KÄSEMANN, *Sätze heiligen Rechts im Neuen Testament*, NTS, I, 1954-1955, 248-260; PH. VIELHAUER, *Gottesreich und Menschensohn in der Verkündigung Jesu*, in *Festschrift für G. Dehn*, Neukirchen, 1957, 51-79; A. Kragerud, *Der Lieblingsjünger im Johannesevangelium*, Oslo, 1959.

CHAPTER IV

THE THEOLOGY OF THE SYNOPTIC GOSPELS

RECENT RESULTS OF TRADITION-CRITICISM suggest that, in considering the actions, message and teaching of Jesus, we should distinguish three levels: the 'historical' level—the level of what Jesus himself said and did, restored to its original form; the level of the tradition of the early Church—the level on which the evangelists are simply passing on to us the earliest kerygma on Jesus, that is, the 'Gospel'; and the level of the evangelists themselves—on which they are setting down their own personal theological ideas within the limits which editorial possibilities allowed them. Although it is difficult to discern and to define these three levels in every case, this distinction is nonetheless a very important one for theology; it is, in fact, the only way we have of distinguishing Jesus' revelation from the theological interpretation of the early Church, and this interpretation from the individual theologies of the evangelists. Hitherto, this distinction has scarcely been attempted in most works on Jesus, or in the corresponding sections in the manuals of New Testament theology; what is more, the problems of history and of theology are generally confused, especially in the numerous 'Lives of Jesus'.[1] But can we really, in actual fact, speak of a 'theology of

[1] On the Protestant side, cf. A. SCHWEITZER, *Geschichte der Leben-Jesu-Forschung 6*, Tubingen, 1951; J. LEIPOLDT, *Vom Jesusbild der Gegenwart 2*,

Jesus'?[1] Can we, short of disregarding the authenticity of the traditions about Jesus, fail to take notice of the interpretation of the early Church, which is patently bound up with them and is even the vehicle through which they are conveyed? Because of the special nature of the Gospels, it is absolutely essential to respect the indissoluble unity of both data, and to opt for a concerted exposition suggested by some such title as 'The message of Jesus according to the Gospel tradition',[2] or, more broadly, 'The saving acts in the life of Jesus according to the synoptic Gospels'. At least, it is permissible to keep the examination of the individual theology of each evangelist for special studies, to be carried out according to the methods of *Redaktionsgeschichte*[3] which is a completely new branch of research.

Leipzig, 1925; J. G. K. HOFFMANN, *Les vies de Jésus et le Jésus de l'histoire*, Paris, 1947; G. LINDESKOG, *Die Jesusfrage im neuzeitlichen Judentum*, Uppsala, 1938; some English works are quoted in W. G. KÜMMEL, *Verheissung und Erfüllung 3*, Zurich, 1956, (English translation 1957).

Among Catholic authors, we might quote A. REATZ, *Jesus Christus, sein Leben, seine Lehre und sein Werk 2*, Freiburg in Br., 1925; M.-J. LAGRANGE, *L'Évangile de Jésus Christ*, Paris, 1928; L. DE GRANDMAISON, *Jésus Christ. Sa personne, son message, ses preuves*, 2 vols., Paris, 1929; F. PRAT, *Jésus-Christ. Sa vie, sa doctrine, son oeuvre*, Paris, 1933 (7, 1938); J. LEBRETON *Jésus-Christ*, Paris, 1931 (German translation 1952), (English translation reprinted 1957); G. RICCIOTTI, *Vita di Gesù Cristo*. 1941 (German translation 2, 1952; French translation 1947); F.-M, BRAUN, *Jésus, Histoire et Critique*, Paris, 1947 (German translation 1950); F. AMIOT, *Vie de Notre-Seigneur Jésus-Christ*, Paris, 1958.

[1] Cf. A. T. CADOUX, *The Theology of Jesus*, London, 1940.

[2] Cf. E. PERCY, *Die Botschaft Jesu. Eine traditionscritische und exegetische Untersuchung*, Lund, 1953; G. BORNKAMM, *Jesus von Nazareth*, Urban-Bücher, 19, Stuttgart, 1956, (English translation 1960).—In the Catholic view, a certain amount of criticism seems to be necessary.

[3] 'Study of the process of editing the Gospels.'

I. THE GENERAL THEOLOGY OF THE SYNOPTIC GOSPELS.

a. The problems.

We have seen that the theology of the synoptic Gospels must be understood as a theological elaboration by the early Church of Jesus' message, teaching, activity and destiny. In all this, immediate interest is aroused by what Jesus said and did. But for any exposition of Jesus' message some theological stand-point is necessary : what elements are essential, central, new, alarming, in this preaching? The proclamation of God's fatherhood and the call for brotherly love towards all men, perhaps?[1] Or a strictly eschatological message, explicable in terms of the external or internal structure of the Judaism of the time, and only erected into a new and enduring religion by the early Church?[2] Or a prophetic and eschatological appeal, summoning every man to make the existential choice of how to understand himself in relation to God and the world?[3]

According to the testimony of the Gospels, Jesus' message and teaching included many elements, and these were intended, practically speaking, just as much for Jesus' contemporaries as for mankind in general, that is, for man as man. If we are seek-ing one central idea which is constantly repeated, and which contains within itself the whole of Jesus' message, we should, along with the majority of contemporary exegetes, choose the proclamation of the approach of the Kingdom of God

---

[1] Cf. A. von HARNACK, *Das Wesen des Christentums*, 1900, *15*, 1950; today, we can find the same stand-point adopted by E. STAUFFER, *Die Botschaft Jesu damals und heute* (*Dalp-Taschenbücher*, 333), Berne, 1959, (English translation 1960).

[2] This view is adopted particularly by A. SCHWEITZER and others of the 'eschatological' school.

[3] This view is held by R. BULTMANN, *Jesus*, Tubingen, 1926, and his disciples.

(Mk. 1.15).[1] And there would be a great deal of justification for this, for in the preaching of the early Church, the message of the 'basileia' lost ground very rapidly in favour of the proclamation of Jesus as Messiah, while the synoptic Gospels continued to bear witness that this was Jesus' principal theme : a situation which already quite obviously posed more than one problem for the early Church.

b. Eschatology.

There are, indeed, a host of theological problems tied to this theme. Jesus' message raises one question of prime importance for the whole of New Testament theology : how are we to interpret the *eschatological* element in it ? Jesus speaks of the imminence of the Kingdom of God, and also presents the 'eschaton' as a reality which is very near in time. What did the early Church understand by this ? And what attitude did she adopt towards it ? Or did she, perhaps, adopt several ? We are not concerned solely with her teaching concerning the last days (see Chapter VIII below); what we want to know is how, starting from Jesus' message, did the early Church regard her own position in salvation-history and, in general terms, how did she see the existence of man and his presence in the world : in other words, what picture did she have of the world, of man and of history ? Today, this is one of the most burning questions in New Testament theology, over which exegetes are split into the supporters of salvation-history, of existentialist theology or of liberal criticism.[2] The choice before us is

[1] Cf. already J. WEISS, *Die Predigt Jesu vom Reiche Gottes 2*, Gottingen, 1900, (he leans towards an eschatological viewpoint); H. H. WENDT, *Die Lehre Jesu 2*, Gottingen, 1901, (traditional). There is a history of interpretations since A. RITSCHL in G. LUNDSTRÖM, *Guds Rike i Jesu förkunnelse*, Lund, 1947 (bibliography); recent works are listed in R. SCHNACKENBURG, *Gottes Herrschaft*, (see p. 44 n. 4, above).

[2] For the extensive literature on eschatological thought, cf. F. HOLMSTRÖM, *Das eschatologische Denken der Gegenwart*, Gutersloh, 1936;

already apparent when we think of the theological judgement we must form on Jesus' message. How are we to understand the 'imminence' of the end which was expected, or, at least, proclaimed? Can we admit that Jesus was mistaken, as quite a few Protestants think? And how did the early Church react to this problem? Did the delay in the Parousia raise serious difficulties, did it even have a decisive influence on the development of early Christianity?[1]

H. D. WENDLAND, *Geschichtsanschauung und Geschichtsbewusstsein im Neuen Testament*, Gottingen, 1938; G. DELLING, *Das Zeitverständnis des Neuen Testaments*, Gutersloh, 1940; O. CULLMANN, *Christus und die Zeit 2*, Zurich, 1948, (English translation 1951); *The Background of the New Testament and its Eschatology*, ed. by W. D. DAVIES and D. DAUBE, *In Honour of C. H. Dodd*, Cambridge, 1956; J. KÖRNER, *Eschatologie und Geschichte*, Hamburg, 1957; R. BULTMANN, *Geschichte und Eschatologie*, Tubingen, 1957, (English translation 1957); G. E. LADD, *Why not Prophetic-Apocalyptic?*, JBL, 76, 1957, 192-200; H. CONZELMANN, *Gegenwart und Zukunft in der synoptischen Tradition*, in *Zeitschrift für Theologie und Kirche*, 54, 1957, 277-296; H. OTT, *Eschatologie*, Zollikon-Zurich, 1958; W. G. KÜMMEL, *op. cit.*, (p. 54 n. 1); ID., *Futurische und präsentische Eschatologie im ältesten Urchristentum*, NTS, 5, 1958-1959, 113-126; R. SCHNACKENBURG, Art. *Eschatologie im Neuen Testament*, in *Lexikon für Theologie und Kirche 2*, vol. 3, Freiburg in Br., 1959, 1088-1093, (bibliog.); among English writers, T. F. GLASSON, *The Second Advent. The Origin of the New Testament Doctrine 2*, London, 1947; J. A. T. ROBINSON, *Jesus and His Coming, the Emergence of a Doctrine*, London, 1957.

[1] Cf. the works by the disciples of A. SCHWEITZER: F. BURI, *Die Bedeutung der neutestamentlichen Eschatologie für die neuere prot. Theologie*, Zurich-Leipzig, 1935; M. WERNER, *Die Entstehung des christlichen Dogmas 2*, Berne, 1953; ID., *Der protestantische Weg des Glaubens*, I, Berne, 1955; in addition to these, see M. STREGE, *Das Eschaton als gestaltende Kraft in der Theologie*, Stuttgart, 1955; E. GRÄSSER, *Das Problem der Parusieverzögerung in den synoptischen Evangelien und in der Apostelgeschichte (Beihefte zur ZNW, 22)*, Berlin, 1957, (bibliog.).—For a criticism of this approach, cf. O. CULLMANN, *Parusieverzögerung und Urchristentum*, in *Theol. Literaturzeitung*, 83, 1958, 1-12; F. J. SCHIERSE, Art. *Eschatologismus*, in *Lexikon für Theologie und Kirche 2*, vol. 3, Freiburg in Br., 1959, 1098 f. (bibliog.); J. GNILKA *'Parusieverzögerung' und Naherwartung in den synopt. Evangelien und in der Apostelgeschichte*, in *Catholica*, 13, 1959, 277-290.

The answer of the early Church—or, better, the answers which are contained in the writings of the New Testament— still await a more careful study. St Paul insists on the tension which characterizes 'Christian existence' in the 'intermediary' period—a tension between the inauguration and the consummation of salvation, between the certainty and the hope of salvation. St John describes the salvation of believers in tones of joy and victory, but he also demands that they should live in charity. There we have two theological replies, and we must have a clear picture of the differences between them, as well as of their profound agreement. The same is true of the eschatology contained in the epistle to the Hebrews, the Catholic epistles and the Apocalypse. All these eschatological tendencies, differing in emphasis, but all convergent, clearly have their roots in Jesus' eschatological message, but the synoptic Gospels themselves in their own way reflect these different attitudes. In any commentary on the Synoptics, it is important to take care to distinguish tradition and interpretation in Jesus' eschatological discourse (Mk. 13 and parallel texts).[1]

c. Ecclesiology.

The synoptic message on the Kingdom also raises an ecclesiological problem. What did the early Church think of herself, in the light of this message? In the context of the approaching Kingdom, what could her meaning be? What could she have to do, if it is true that the Kingdom, although not yet present in glory, is nonetheless inaugurated and, as it were, provisionally established? What could the relationship be between the

---

[1] Cf. W. G. KÜMMEL, op. cit., (2nd ed. 88-97); G. R. BEASLEY-MURRAY, Jesus and the Future, London, 1954, (bibliog.); ID., A Commentary on Mark XIII, London, 1957; on the Catholic side, cf. especially the commentaries by J. SCHMID in Regensburger NT.

Church which Jesus founded on earth, and the Kingdom of God which he proclaimed and inaugurated? This is obviously not just a matter of the historical problem of Jesus' foundation of the Church, but of very serious theological problems, which might be formulated under the following heads : 'Jesus and the Church', 'The Kingdom of God and the Church', 'The proclamation and the realization of salvation'. We should like to see Catholic studies on these questions, taking the present state of research into account, and pointing the way towards theological solutions.[1]

d. Christology.

The christological question is still acute : what did Jesus think of himself, and what did he reveal about himself? In this instance, there is no lack of Catholic works,[2] but too often they are apologetic in character, and do not try hard enough to start from the actual affirmations of the New Testament—or, for example, from the declarations of the ancient prophets to which Jesus reverted—in order to discover what in Jesus' messianic consciousness is unique and original. But do we therefore have to admit that Jesus looked upon himself as a prophet, albeit an eminent one?[3] To what extent was his mind steeped

[1] Cf. F.-M. Braun, *Aspects nouveaux du problème de l'Église*, Fribourg (Switzerland) 1942: in German: *Neues Licht auf die Kirche*, Einsiedeln-Cologne, 1946 (bibliog.); L. Kösters, *Die Kirche unseres Glaubens 4*, Freiburg in Br., 1952, (bibliog.); A. Medebielle, in DBS, II, 487-691 (bibliog.).

[2] See especially L. de Grandmaison, *op. cit.* (and the abridged edition, Paris, 1957); H. Felder, *Jesus von Nazareth 3*, Paderborn, 1949; L. Kösters, *Unsere Christusglaube 2*, Freiburg in Br., 1939; K. Adam, *Jesus-Christus 8*, Dusseldorf, 1950; *Lumière et Vie*, 9, 1953.

[3] Cf. F. Gils, *Jésus Prophète d'après les Évangiles Synoptiques (Orientalia et Biblica Lovaniensia*, II), Louvain, 1957; there is a complete bibliography in TW, VII, 781-783; G. Friedrich, on Jesus, *ibidem*, 842-849.

in Ebed Yahweh[1] (deutero-Isaiah)?[2] What did he consider
the role of the 'Son of Man' to be?[3] How are we to interpret
the title 'Son of God', both in the witness which he gives of
himself and in the interpretation of the early Church?[4] Even
those who refuse to admit that Jesus knew he was the Messiah,
or who think that there is nothing certain they can say on the
subject,[5] build up a picture of Jesus for themselves, and force us
to compare it with our own.

e. Morality and the Christian life.

Nor can we neglect Jesus' moral message either—so intimately bound up as it is with his preaching on the Kingdom. This

---

[1] 'The Servant of Yahweh'.

[2] Bibliography up to 1954, in TW, V, 653-655; J. JEREMIAS, on
Jesus, ibidem, 698-703, 709-713; next cf. T. W. MANSON, The Servant-
Messiah, London, 1953; CH. MAURER, Knecht Gottes und Sohn Gottes im
Passionsbericht des Markusevangeliums, in Zeitschrift für Theologie und
Kirche, 50, 1953, 1-38; E. SCHWEIZER, Erniedrigung und Erhöhung bei
Jesus und seinen Nachfolgern, in Abhandlungen zur Theologie des Alten und
Neuen Testaments, 28, Zurich, 1955, 81-86; E. LOHSE, Märtyrer und
Gottesknecht, Gottingen, 1955; O. CULLMANN, Christologie, 50-81; J. N.
SEVENSTER, Jezus en de Ebed Jahwe, in Nederl. Theol. Tijdschrift, 13, 1958,
27-46; J. L. PRICE, The Servant Motive in the Synoptic Gospels, in Interpreta-
tion, 1958, 28-38; F. MUSSNER, in Lexikon für Theologie und Kirche 2,
vol. 3, Freiburg in Br., 1959, 624f.

[3] Cf. Chapter III, p. 52 n. 3, above.

[4] Cf. Chapter III, p. 52 n. 3, above; in addition, see the literature on
Mt. 11, 25-30, especially T. ARVEDSON, Das Mysterium Christi, Uppsala-
Leipzig, 1937; L. CERFAUX, Les sources scripturaires de Mt. 11, 25-30, in
Ephem. Theol. Lovan., 30, 1954, 740-746; 31, 1955, 331-342; A. FEUILLET,
Jésus et la Sagesse divine d'après les Évangiles Synoptiques, RB, 62, 1955,
161-196; H. MERTENS, L'hymne de jubilation chez les Synoptiques (Diss. de la
Grégorienne, 1954), Gembloux, 1957; S. LEGASSE, La révélation aux
NHΠIOI, RB, 67, 1960, 321-348.

[5] This is true at the moment of many of the representatives of the
school of 'Form-criticism' (Bultmann, Bornkamm, Vielhauer, etc.).
For the opposite view, cf. W. MANSON, Jesus the Messiah, London, 1943
(German translation 1952); R. H. FULLER, The Mission and Achievement
of Jesus (Studies in Bibl. Theol. 12), London, 1954; E. SJÖBERG, Der
verborgene Menschensohn (see Chapter III, p. 52 n. 3).

message is given various interpretations today—socialist,[1] existentialist,[2] and humanitarian.[3] There are not many Catholic works, exegetically based, on Jesus' moral teaching,[4] although we do possess valuable monographs dealing, for example, with the idea of reward in Jesus' teaching,[5] with the beatitudes,[6] the idea of poverty,[7] Jesus' attitude to women[8] and to marriage.[9] Scarcely any Catholic authors have taken part in the burning controversy over Jesus' attitude to the State.[10]

[1] Cf. L. RAGAZ, Die Bergpredigt, Berne, 1945.

[2] Cf. R. BULTMANN, Jesus; E. FUCHS, Die vollkommene Gewissheit. Zur Auslegung von Mt 5. 48, in Neutestamentliche Studien für R. Bultmann, Berlin, 1954, 130-136; G. BORNKAMM, op. cit.

[3] Cf. E. STAUFFER, Die Botschaft Jesu damals und heute (Dalp-Taschenbücher, 333), Berne-Munich, 1959.

[4] M.-J. LAGRANGE, La morale de l'Évangile, Paris, 1931; J. HERKENRATH, Die Ethik Jesu in ihren Grundzügen, Dusseldorf, 1926; B. LANWER, Die Grundgedanken der Bergpredigt auf dem Hintergrund des Alten Testamentes und des Spätjudentums, Hiltrup, 1934; TH. SOIRON, Die Bergpredigt Jesu, Freiburg in Br., 1944; A. DESCAMPS, La morale des synoptiques, in Morale chrétienne et requêtes contemporaines, Tournai-Paris, 1954, 27-46. There is more information further on, Chapter VIII, section 4.

[5] W. PESCH, Der Lohngedanke in der Lehre Jesu vergleichen mit der religiösen Lohnlehre des Spätjudentums (Münchener Theol. Studien, I, 7), Munich, 1955 (bibliog.).

[6] J. DUPONT, Les Béatitudes, Bruges-Louvain, 1954; a completely revised new edition: I. Le problème littéraire, 1958.

[7] A. CAUSSE, Les pauvres d'Israël, Paris, 1922; J. VAN DER PLOEG, Les pauvres d'Israel et leur piété, in Oudtestam. Studien, 7, 1950, 236-270; A. GELIN, Les Pauvres de Yahvé 2, Paris, 1953; E. PERCY, Die Botschaft Jesu, 45-81; ST. J. PIAT, L'Évangile de la pauvreté, Paris, 1956.

[8] P. KETTER, Christus und die Frauen, 2 vols., Stuttgart, 1944-1949.

[9] J. FISCHER, Ehe und Jungfräulichkeit im Neuen Testament, Munster-in-W., 1919; J. BONSIRVEN, Le divorce dans le Nouveau Testament, Tournai-Paris, 1948; H. CAZELLES, Mariage, DBS, V, 1957, 926-935 (bibliog.); J. DUPONT, Mariage et divorce dans l'Évangile, Bruges, 1959. On virginity, cf. J. BLINZLER, Εἰσὶν εὐνοῦχοι. Zur Auslegung von Mt. 19. 12, ZNW, 48, 1957, 254-270.

[10] Cf. the discussion of the question by W. G. KÜMMEL, in Theol. Rundschau, 17, 1948, 133-142; in addition, see W. SCHWEITZER, Die Herrschaft Christi und der Staat im Neuen Testament, Munich, 1949; O. CULLMANN, Der Staat im Neuen Testament, Tubingen, 1956 (English translation 1957); E. STAUFFER, Botschaft Jesu, 95-118.

More immediately *religious* themes—such as our access to the Father in Jesus, Jesus' teaching on prayer and his attitude to the liturgy—have been no better treated. And where are we to find a Catholic monograph on the Lord's Prayer[1] or on worship in spirit and in truth (Jn. 4.23 ff)? The early Church made up for what was lacking in Jesus' words by its actions—actions which were faithful to Jesus' mind and which had been prompted by the Holy Spirit. The summit of its worship was the celebration of the Eucharist. It is pleasant to be able to say the theological significance of Jesus' institution of the Eucharist has been better revealed,[2] and this time, moreover, in fruitful dialogue with Protestant research.[3]

f. The interpretation of history.

This brings us to the threshold of the study of Jesus' activity and destiny. We cannot separate his message from his history; on the contrary, we have to interpret what Jesus did and suffered in the light of what he said about it. This was precisely

[1] But cf. H. SCHÜRMANN, *Das Gebet des Herrn,* in *Die Botschaft Gottes,* II, 6, Leipzig; 1957; H. VAN DEN BUSSCHE, *Le Notre Père, Études religieuses,* Brussels-Paris, 1960; on the Protestant side, cf. especially E. LOHMEYER, *Das Vaterunser 3,* Gottingen, 1952 (bibliog.).

[2] W. GOOSSENS, *Les origines de l'Eucharistie. Sacrement et sacrifice,* Gembloux-Paris, 1931; A. ARNOLD, *Der Ursprung des christlichen Abendmahls im Lichte der neuesten liturgiegeschichtlichen Forschung,* Freiburg in Br., 1937; H. SCHÜRMANN, *Der Paschalmahlbericht Lk. 22, (7-14) 15-18* (*Neutest. Abh.,* XIX, 5), Munster-in-W., 1953; *Der Einsetzungsbericht Lk. 22, 19-20* (*Neutest. Abh.,* XX, 4), 1955; *Jesu Abschiedsrede Lk. 22. 21-38* (*Neutest. Abh.,* XX, 5), 1957 (bibliog.); ID., Art. *Abendmahl.* in *Lexikon für Theologie und Kirche 2,* vol. 1, Freiburg in Br., 1957, 26-31 (bibliog.); *Lumière et Vie,* 31, 1957. Cf. P. NEUENZEIT, *op. cit.* below (Chapter V, p. 87 n. 1).

[3] There is a bulletin on the state of research by E. LOHMEYER in *Theol. Rundschau,* 9, 1937; E. SCHWEIZER, in *Theol. Literaturzeitung,* 79, 1954, 577-592; H. LESSIG, *Das Abendmahlsproblem im Lichte der neutestamentlichen Forschung seit* 1900 (Diss. Bonn, 1953, unpublished); in addition, see especially J. JEREMIAS, *Die Abendmahlsworte Jesu 3,* Gottingen, 1960 (bibliog.).

the concern of the early Church, after the Resurrection, as we can see already, not only in the summaries in the discourses in Acts (Acts 2.22 ff.; 3.13 ff.; 10.37-39; 13.23-25, 27-30), but also, and most particularly, in the choice and the form of the narrative pericopes in the Gospels. On this point, form-criticism has contributed a great deal, although we are forced to reject its assessment of the historical value of the narrations.[1] There is still no exhaustive examination of the Gospel texts, conducted from this point of view, by a Catholic; but we can obtain an idea of what this sort of theological approach would be like from R. Laurentin's exemplary study of Luke 1-2[2]— although we might differ from him on certain points. What we have to do is to discern the 'kerygmatic' character of the narra-tion, and, in order to do this, to take the 'Sitz im Leben' of the early Church into account; we have to grasp the 'scriptural theology' (the Old Testament background) which the early Church had already developed, and which here provides the narrative with its thread and its colouring. This is something which W. Hillmann and K. H. Schelkle have brought to our notice with regard to the Passion account.[3]

But other sectors of the synoptic tradition also need to be studied in this way. There are very many narrations which throw a vivid light on the depths of Jesus' personality—his baptism, his temptation, his walking on the waters and his

[1] Cf. E. Schick, *Formgeschichte und Synoptikerexegese* (*Neutest. Abh.* XVIII, 2-3), Munster-in-W., 1940; A. Wikenhauser, *Einleitung in das Neue Testament 1*, Freiburg in Br., 1956, 182-199 (bibliog.); J. Cambier, *Historicité des évangiles et Formgeschichte*, in *La Formation des Évangiles* (*Recherches Bibliques*, 2), Louvain, 1957, 195-212; X. Leon-Dufour, *Formgeschichte und Redaktionsgeschichte du Nouveau Testament* (Bulletin), in *Recherches de Science Religieuse*, 46, 1958, 237-269.

[2] R. Laurentin, *Structure et théologie de Luc I-II* (*Études Bibliques*), Paris, 1957.

[3] W. Hillmann, *Aufbau und Deutung der synoptischen Leidensberichte*, Freiburg in Br., 1941; K. H. Schelkle, *op. cit.*

transfiguration—and which belong to a very special type of histories of Christ.[1] Jesus' healing and miracles are something more than a simple proof of his divinity.[2] Seen at its deepest level, the whole of John's Gospel—by its insistence on 'signs'— is simply one long illustration of the kerygmatic understanding of Jesus' history in the early Church; and, although it is more difficult to recognize, a similar vision dominates the synoptic Gospels as well. We can say that, without disturbing the level of history—the level of Jesus' activity, which is vouched for by the eye-witnesses and by those who listened to them—the events narrated are charged with a more profound theological meaning, which the early Church brought out in its catechesis. In the same way, the sections which tell of controversies (Mk. 2.1-3.6), teaching (Mk. 12.1-45) or discussions (as in Mk. 12.13-37),[3] should be further explained with reference to the catechetical vision of the early Church. Even the general unfolding of Christ's active life, with its tensions between faith

---

[1] On Jesus' temptation, Cf. R. SCHNACKENBURG, *Der Sinn der Versuchung Jesu bei den Synoptikern*, in *Theol. Quartalschrift*, 132, 1952, 297-326 (bibliog.); M. SABBE, *De tentatione Jesu in deserto*, in *Collationes Brugenses*, 50, 1954, 200-222; J. DUPONT, *L'arrière-fond biblique du récit des tentations de Jésus*, NTS, 3, 1956-1957, 287-304. On the Transfiguration, cf. J. BLINZLER, *Die neutestam. Berichte über die Verklärung Jesu* (*Neutest. Abh.* XVII, 4), Munster-in-W., 1937; J. HÖLLER, *Die Verklärung Jesu*, Freiburg in Br., 1937; E. DABROWSKI, *La transfiguration de Jésus*, Rome, 1939; H. RIESENFELD, *Jésus transfiguré*, Copenhagen, 1947; B. ZIELINSKI, *De transfigurationis sensu*, in *Verbum Domini*, 26, 1948, 335-343; A. M. RAMSAY, *The Glory of God and the Transfiguration of Christ*, London, 1949; H. BALTENSWEILER, *Die Verklärung Jesu* (*Abhandl. z. Theol. des A. und N.T.*, 33), Zurich, 1959.

[2] Cf. L. DE GRANDMAISON, *Jésus Christ*, II, 330-368; A. RICHARDSON, *The Miracle-Stories of the Gospels*, London, 1941; G. DELLING, *Das Verständnis des Wunders im Neuen Testament*, in *Zeitschrift für systematische Theologie*, 24, 1955, 265-280.

[3] Cf. D. DAUBE, *The New Testament and Rabbinic Judaism*, London, 1956, 158-169; ID., *The Earliest Structure of the Gospels*, NTS, 5, 1958-1959, 174-187 (he puts forward the hypothesis of a Christian haggadah on the Pasch).

3

and incredulity, was looked upon by the early Church as a revelation of God's plan for salvation, as Jesus himself had shown from time to time (cf. Mt. 11.25-27 and parallels; Mk. 4.11 ff and parallels; Lk. 12.32; 22.28-30; Mk. 10.45; 14.24 and parallels). It is not enough to pay attention to the 'pedagogy' implied in the fact that Jesus progressively unfolds revelation and teaching:[1] we must also, along with the early Church, understand Jesus' life within the plan of salvation. We do have some works which follow these lines,[2] but, in general, studies on Jesus have not yet adopted this standpoint.

2. THE INDIVIDUAL THEOLOGY OF THE SYNOPTICS

In a more or less conscious reaction to some of the one-sided conclusions of 'Form-criticism', there has recently grown up a conviction that the evangelists did have enough freedom, within the framework of their editing of traditional material, by ordering or connecting the pericopes, and by grouping and formulating Jesus' words and discourses, to express their own theological ideas in their own way. For this reason, an interest in the individual theologies of Mark, Luke and Matthew has revived. Although works along these lines have so far been few they have nonetheless proved to be remarkable.

a. St Luke.

The first work was H. Conzelmann's study of Luke's theology.[3] Pursuing the aim which we have just mentioned—that is,

---

[1] Cf. J. BONSIRVEN, *Les enseignements de Jésus*, Paris, 1946.

[2] V. TAYLOR, *Jesus and His Sacrifice*, London, 1957; G. S. DUNCAN, *Jesus, Son of Man*, London, 1948; R. H. FULLER, *op. cit.* (p. 61 n. 5); W. GRUNDMANN, *Die Geschichte Jesu Christi*, Berlin, 1957.

[3] H. CONZELMANN, *Die Mitte der Zeit, Studien zur Theologie des Lukas 3* (*Beiträge zur historischen Theologie*, 17), Tubingen, 1960 (English translation London 1960).

research into the evangelist's own point of view—the author examines the geographical data (there were already some preparatory works on this subject),[1] eschatology, the salvific action of God in history, the life of Jesus as the 'centre of time', and the meaning of the Church. In his introduction, he summarizes Luke's theological contribution in these words: 'The period of Jesus and the period of the Church are presented as different epochs in the broad course of saving history, differentiated to some extent by their particular characteristics' (p. 13); 'Luke is confronted by the situation in which the Church finds herself by the delay of the Parousia and her existence in secular history, and he tries to come to terms with the situation by his account of historical events' (p. 14). If it is true that Conzelmann puts forward quite a few debatable assertions, he has still clearly seen that Luke became the 'theologian of salvation-history'.[2] But we must certainly doubt whether the author of the third Gospel adopted a completely novel position on the eschatological question, a position on quite different lines from that of the early Church.[3] However, in the main, this method helps us to a better knowledge of Luke's double work.

---

[1] R. H. LIGHTFOOT, *History and Interpretation in the Gospels*, London, 1935; E. LOHMEYER, *Galiläa und Jerusalem* (*Forschungen zur Religion und Literatur des Alten und Neuen Testaments*, 52), Gottingen, 1936; cf. also J. BLINZLER, *Die literarische Eigenart des sog. Reiseberichts im Lukasevangelium*, in *Synoptische Studien, Festschrift für A. Wikenhauser*, Munich, 1954, 20-52; J. SCHNEIDER, *Zur Analyse des lukanischen Reiseberichtes, op. cit.*, 207-229; W. M. C. ROBINSON, *The Theological Concept for Interpreting Luke's Travel Narrative*, JBL, 79, 1960, 20-31.

[2] Cf. also E. LOHSE, *Lukas als Theologe der Heilsgeschichte* in *Evangelische Theologie*, 14, 1954, 256-275.

[3] Cf. P. BORGEN, *Eschatology and Redemptive History in Luke-Acts* (Diss.), Oslo, 1957; R. SCHNACKENBURG, *Gottes Herrschaft*, 94-96; 189-194; cf. also U. LUCK, *Kerygma, Tradition und Geschichte Jesu bei Lukas*, in *Zeitschrift für Theologie und Kirche*, 57, 1960, 51-66

b. St Mark.

In the case of Mark's Gospel, W. Marxsen has devoted a *redaktionsgeschichtlich* study to him, which he introduces with methodological considerations on the theme of *Formgeschichte und Redaktionsgeschichte*.[1] His book does not provide us with a complete theology of Mark: above all, the christology of the Son of Man and of the messianic secret are missing. The author is content to bring out Mark's form of four great themes: John the Baptist, the geographical setting, the 'Gospel', and the eschatological discourse (Mk. 13). The thesis which he argues holds good, in fact, for all the Gospels: 'The traditional material has been reworked and adapted to the immediate situation'.[2] Mark's topographical views and their background have also been studied by G. Schille,[3] and Mark's conception of history by J. M. Robinson, in a valuable little work.[4]

c. St Matthew.

There is a Catholic work on the Gospel of St Matthew— W. Trilling's dissertation (Munich).[5] The author has very rightly seen the central importance for New Testament theology of the attitude adopted by this Judeo-Christian evangelist towards

---

[1] W. MARXSEN, *Der Evangelist Markus, Studien zur Redaktionsgeschichte des Evangeliums (Forschungen zur Religion und Literatur des Alten und Neuen Testaments,* 67), Gottingen, 1956; cf. also H. RIESENFELD, *Tradition und Redaktion im Markusevangelium,* in *Neutestamentliche Studien für R. Bultmann,* Berlin, 1954, 157-164.

[2] *Op. cit.,* 139.

[3] G. SCHILLE, *Die Topographie des Markusevangeliums, ihre Hintergründe und ihre Einordnung,* in *Zeitschrift des Deutschen Palästina-Vereins,* 73, 1957, 133-166.

[4] J. M. ROBINSON, *The Problem of History in Mark (Studies in Biblical Theology,* 21), London, 1957; German translation 1956; cf. also T. A. BURKILL, *St Mark's Philosophy of History,* NTS, 3, 1956-1957, 142-148; ID., *St Mark's Philosophy of the Passion,* NT, 2, 1958, 245-271.

[5] W. TRILLING, *Das wahre Israel. Studien zur Theologie des Matthäusevangeliums,* Leipzig, 1959.

Israel. He examines, with penetrating analysis, crowned by a theological synthesis, the Judgement of Israel (the empirical Israel), as well as the constitution of the true Israel and of its Torah. In so doing, he renews our knowledge of the 'sense of the Church' which belongs especially to Matthew, and shows how this special characteristic was conditioned by controversy with the former chosen people. There have been Protestant studies dealing with 'the expectation of the end of the world, and the Church in Matthew's Gospel',[1] with Matthew's account of the Passion,[2] 'the understanding of the Law in Matthew's Gospel', 'Matthew, the interpreter of the miracle narratives',[3] and 'the way of justice'.[4] But it is pleasant to note that Catholic scholarship has also been quick to recognize the importance and the interest of a theological analysis of each individual Synoptic.[5]

At the same time, these studies have renewed the problem of Form- and Tradition-criticism. Fresh researches into the 'Sitz im Leben' of each of the Gospels are urgently required, and it is going to be necessary to shed some of our preconceived notions.[6] It seems that progress in the theology of the Synoptics

---

[1] G. BORNKAMM, *Enderwartung und Kirche im Matthäusevangelium* in *In Honour of C. H. Dodd*, (p. 57 n. 2 above), 222-260.

[2] N. A. DAHL, *Die Passionsgeschichte bei Matthäus*, NTS, 2, 1955-1956, 17-32.

[3] G. BORNKAMM, G. BARTH, H. J. HELD, *Überlieferung und Auslegung im Matthäusevangelium*, Neukirchen, 1960.

[4] G. STRECKER, *Der Weg der Gerechtigkeit, Untersuchungen über den Evangelisten Matthäus, evang. Habilitationsschrift*, Bonn, 1959; cf. *Theol. Literaturzeitung*, 84, 1959, 548; on the Catholic side: A. DESCAMPS, *Les justes et la Justice dans les Évangiles* (*Diss. Lov.*, II, 43), Louvain, 1950.

[5] Cf. X. LEON-DUFOUR, *loc. cit.* (p. 64 n. 1 above); L. GNILKA, *Die Verstockung Israels, Is 6.9 s. in der Theologie der Synoptiker* (*Studien zum Alten und Neuen Testament*, 3), Munich, 1961.

[6] Cf. G. IBER, *Zur Formgeschichte der Evangelien*, in *Theol. Rundschau*, 24, 1956-1957, 283-338; K. STENDAHL, *The School of St. Matthew*, Uppsala, 1954; ID., *Implications of Form-Criticism and Tradition-Criticism for*

will not be possible without constant attention to the special characteristics which the history of the synoptic tradition displays.

Biblical Interpretation, JBL, 77, 1958, 33-38; H. RIESENFELD, *The Gospel Tradition and its Beginnings*, London, 1957; G. SCHILLE, *Bemerkungen zur Formgeschichte des Evangeliums*, NTS, 4, 1957-1958, 1-24, 101-114; 5, 1958-1959, 1-11; D. M. STANLEY, *Liturgical Influences on the Formation of the Four Gospels*, CBQ, 21, 1959, 24-38.

CHAPTER V

THE THEOLOGY OF ST PAUL

I. GENERAL QUESTIONS

PAUL, A GREAT THINKER, intensely moved by the experience of his contact with Christ, has left us a body of teaching both full and profound, although the audacious and paradoxical manner of its expression makes it difficult to interpret. In recent years it has not been left to Lutheran theology—which looks particularly to Paul for its authority—to concentrate attention on the Apostle's ideas: all who hope for a living, existentialist theology, capable of fully satisfying the deepest aspirations, are increasingly attracted by it.

Once again, there is no agreement in principle on the way in which this religious genius should be interpreted. Are we to approach Paul, a product of the Judaism of the Dispersion, who had received a Rabbinical training at Jerusalem, from the basis of Palestinian Pharisaism,[1] Hellenistic Judaism[2]—or even

---

[1] Cf. W. D. DAVIES, *Paul and Rabbinic Judaism 2*, London, 1955.
[2] Cf. C. G. MONTEFIORE, *Judaism and St. Paul*, London, 1914; A. DEISSMANN, *Paulus 2*, Tubingen, 1925 (Paul as a 'Septuagint-Jew'!) (English translation reprinted 1959); H. WINDISCH, *Paulus und das Judentum*, Stuttgart, 1935; J. KLAUSNER, *From Jesus to Paul*, London, 1944 (German translation 1950).

Hellenistic paganism?[1] Did Paul the Christian remain a Jew in his judgements and feelings, despite his break with the religion of his fathers? Or was he, both as missionary and as theologian, the forerunner of Christian Hellenism, the man responsible for the fusion between faith in Christ and the pagan world of mystery religions, mysticism and gnosis? Was his devotion to Christ, branded by the influence of his experience at Damascus,[2] eschatological, mystical or both?[3] Was his thought *heilsgeschichtlich*, dialectical, or even existentialist? There is no simple general answer to these questions.[4] But

---

[1] This view was adopted by the old history of religion school (A. Dieterich, R. Reitzenstein, W. Bousset, W. Heitmüller and others), and has been taken up again recently by C. Schneider, *Geistesgeschichte des antiken Christentums*, 2 vols., Munich, 1954 (see, on this point, the review by E. Stommel in *Jahrbuch für Antike und Christentum*, I, Munster-in-W, 1958, 119-127). For criticism from the Catholic side, K. Prümm, *op. cit.*, (Chapter II, p. 32 n. 3); J. Dey, Παλιγγενεσία (*Neutest. Abh.*, XVIII, 5) Munster-in-W., 1937; J. Dupont, *Gnosis. La connaissance religieuse dans les épîtres de saint Paul*, (Diss. Lovan., II, 40), Louvain, 1949; R. Follet-K. Prümm, Art. *Mystères*, DBS, VI, 1957, 1-225.

[2] Cf. E. Pfaff, *Dei Bekehrung des Paulus in der Exegese des 20 Jahrhunderts*, Rome, 1942 (bibliog.); J. Munck, *La vocation de l'Apôtre Paul*, in *Studia Theologica*, I, 1947, 131-145; Ph. H. Menoud, *Révélation et Tradition. L'influence de la conversion de Paul sur sa théologie*, in *Verbum Caro*, 7, 1953, 2-10; G. H. Wood, *The Conversion of St. Paul*, NTS, I, 1955-1956, 276-282; W. Prokulski, *The Conversion of St. Paul*, CBQ, 19, 1957, 453-473; A.-M. Denis, *L'élection et la vocation de Paul, faveurs célestes*, in *Revue Thomiste*, 57, 1957, 405-428; H. J. Schoeps, *Paulus. Die Theologie des Apostels im Lichte der jüdischen Religionsgeschichte*, Tubingen, 1959, 46-52, (English translation 1960).

[3] For the history of the 'Forschung', cf. A. Schweitzer, *Geschichte der paulinischen Forschung von der Reformation bis auf die Gegenwart*, Tubingen, 1911 (=2nd ed. 1933); R. Bultmann, *Neueste Paulusforschung*, in *Theol. Rundschau*, 6, 1934, 229-246; 8, 1936, 1-22; A.-M. Denis, *Saint Paul dans la littérature récente*, in *Ephemerides Theol. Lovanienses*, 26, 1950, 383-394; J. Coppens, *L'état présent des études pauliniennes*, art. cit., 32, 1956, 363-372; in addition, cf the bulletins of the *Revue des Sciences Philos. et Théol.*; B. Rigaux, *L'interprétation du paulinisme dans l'exégèse récente*, in *Littérature et Théologie paulinienne* (*Recherches bibliques*, 5), Paris, 1960, 17-46.

[4] Cf. Schoeps, *op. cit.*, 1-42.

since Paul was every inch a theologian, and saw even the most worldly realities in the light of his religious thought, it is utterly impossible to separate his theology from his personality. Not only the biographies of Paul,[1] but also the studies of his theology, must take this into account, and faced with his frequent apparently contradictory statements, must never lose sight of the man Paul and of his dynamic and passionate soul.

In the following survey, whose primary purpose is to provide us with our general bearings, we shall be able to dwell on only a few of the problems of his theology—those which are at the centre of current debates. In addition to the manuals of New Testament theology, which often assign a large place to Paul, we possess several Catholic works on the whole body of Pauline theology : F. Prat's two fine volumes[2] (which are packed with material, although they are now out of date on more than one point) and the works by L. Tondelli,[3] F. Amiot[4] and J. Bonsirven.[5] Among Protestant authors, we should mention E. Lohmeyer,[6] A. Schweitzer[7] and, from a Jewish point of view,

---

[1] There is an outline by C. Toussaint, in SDB, IV 2, Paris, 1928, 2188-2231; R. Bultmann, in *Theol. Rundschau*, I, 1929, 26-59; P. Feine, *Der Apostel Paulus. Das Ringen um das geschichtliche Verständnis des Paulus*, Gutersloh, 1927.—Catholic treatments: K. Peiper, *Paulus, seine missionarische Persönlichkeit and Wirksamkeit 2*, (*Neutest. Abh.*, XII, 1-2), Munster-in-W., 1929; E. B. Allo, *Paul, Apôtre de Jésus-Christ*, Paris, 1942; G. Ricciotti, *Paolo Apostolo*, Rome, 1946; German translation, 1950; French translation 1952; A. Brunot, *Saint Paul et son message*, Paris, 1958, (English translation 1959); J. Perez de Urbel, *Saint Paul, sa vie et son temps*, Paris, 1958; N. Caserta, *Il Dottore delle Genti*, Rome, 1958.

[2] F. Prat, *La théologie de saint Paul 38*, 2 vols., Paris, 1949, (English translation reprinted in one volume 1957).

[3] L. Tondelli, *Il Pensiero di S. Paolo 2*, Turin, 1948.

[4] F. Amiot, *L'enseignement de saint Paul 4*, 2 vols., Paris, 1946.

[5] J. Bonsirven, *L'évangile de Paul*, Paris, 1948.

[6] E. Lohmeyer, *Grundlagen paulinischer Theologie* (*Beiträge zur historischen Theologie*, I), Tubingen, 1929.

[7] A. Schweitzer, *Die Mystik des Apostels Paulus*, Tubingen, 1930 (=2nd ed. 1954) (English translation 1953).

H. J. Schoeps,[1] to say nothing of numerous individual studies. It is not possible to extract a complete theological system from St Paul, because of the fragmentary character of the themes which he introduces in his epistles; but there are certain main lines which stand out clearly.[2]

2. CHRISTOLOGY AND SOTERIOLOGY.

There can be no doubt that Paul's theology is *christocentric* : even the teaching about God on which this 'theology' is largely based, as we can see particularly in the 'theodicy' of Rom. 9-11,[3] bears the imprint of Christ : it is the 'Father of our Lord Jesus Christ' (2 Cor. 1.3; Eph. 1.3; Col. 1.3), who has formed and carried out the plan of saving us in Christ (Eph. 1.3-14),[4] and it is for this that the community thanks him (Rom. 5.11; 7.25; 11. 33-36; Phil. 2.11 etc.). But Paul's christology bears the imprint of his soteriology : his central preoccupation is the salvation of man and Christ's reconciliation of the world. Redemption through the cross of Christ lies at the heart of Paul's thought—a redemption which God, in his mercy, gives all mankind, fallen into sin and death (cf. 1 Cor. 1.18-2.9; Rom. 3. 21-26). So much is this so that, before this truth, the words and actions of the man Jesus fade completely into the

---

[1] *Op. cit.*, (p. 72 n. 2).

[2] Cf. F. W. MAIER, Art. *Paulus*, in *Lexikon für Theologie und Kirche*, vol. 8, Freiburg in Br., 1936, 27-43, here 34-40.

[3] F. W. MAIER, *Israel in der Heilsgeschichte nach Röm 9-11*, Munster-in-W., 1929; J. MUNCK, *Christus und Israel. Eine Auslegung von Röm 9-11*, Copenhagen, 1956; S. LYONNET, *Quaestiones in Epistulam ad Romanos*, II, Rome, 1956 (bibliog); E. DINKLER, *Prädestination bei Paulus, Festschrift G. Dehn*, Neukirchen, 1957, 81-102.

[4] Cf. L. G. CHAMPION, *Benedictions and Doxologies in the Epistles of Paul* (Diss.), Heidelberg, 1934; P. SCHUBERT, *Form and Function of the Pauline Thanksgivings*, Berlin, 1939; H. SCHLIER, *Der Brief an die Epheser*, Dusseldorf, 1957, 38-74.

background. Paul's christology[1] is confined to the Son of God, who was sent to us by the Father when the times were fulfilled (Gal. 4.4; cf. Rom. 8.32), to the crucified and risen Christ, and to the Lord who is now living in heaven and who will soon come in glory (Col. 3.1-4; Phil. 3.20 ff.) for the good of mankind and of the world, to complete the work of salvation (cf. 1 Cor. 15.24-28; Rom. 8.19-23). It follows that his teaching on salvation is also markedly eschatological (cf. Rom. 8.24).

Paul's soteriology, which embraces the whole world,[2] needs clarification on more than one point—on the question of its cosmic import (cf. Col. 1.20), for example;[3] we can say, however, that it always has been the object of a great deal of interest, along with the subjective soteriology which goes with it (justification by faith, baptism and morality). But it is based on certain presuppositions and these are what claim attention today.

The first is 'natural theology', that is to say, the 'revelation' of God in creation and the natural knowledge of God. Is the speech in the Areopagus (Acts 17), at least in its essential lines, really so untypically Pauline as critics have long believed?[4]

---

[1] L. CERFAUX, Le Christ dans la théologie de saint Paul (Lectio divina, 6), Paris, 1951 (English translation 1959).—For other works on christology, see Chapter VIII, section 1 below.

[2] R. G. BANDAS, The Master-Idea of St. Paul's Epistles or the Redemption (Diss. Lovan.), Bruges, 1925; G. WIENCKE, Paulus über Jesu Tod, Gutersloh, 1939; PH. SEIDENSTICKER, Lebendiges Opfer (Rom. 12.1) (Neutest. Abh. XX, 1-3), Munster-en-W., 1954, (bibliog.).

[3] Cf. E. TESTA, Gesù pacificatore universale, Assisi, 1956.

[4] Cf. M. POHLENZ, Paulus und die Stoa, ZNW, 42, 1949, 69-104; A. LACKMANN, Vom Geheimnis der Schöpfung, Stuttgart, 1952; B. GÄRTNER, The Areopagus Speech and Natural Revelation, Uppsala 1955 (bibliog.); W. NAUCK, Die Tradition und Komposition der Areopagrede, in Zeitschrift für Theologie und Kirche, 53, 1956, 11-52; W. ELTESTER, Schöpfungsoffenbarung und natürliche Theologie im frühen Christentum, NTS, 3, 1956-1957, 93-114; H. P. OWEN, The Scope of Natural Revelation in Rom. I and Acts XVII, NTS, 5, 1958-1959; 133-143.

Surely, in Rom. 1.18-32, Paul had already used themes typical
of the missionary preaching of Hellenistic Judaism,[1] even if he
rejects the idea that the light of natural intelligence (Rom. 1.20)
and the 'wisdom of this world' (1 Cor. 1.19-21; 2.6) have
opened for man the way to salvation. This question, like that
of the moral law which pagans discover in their consciences
(Rom. 2.14-16),[2] will be discussed again later; in fact, his
eschatological views on the transformation of the world pre-
suppose a preliminary 'revelation' in creation; man renewed
in Christ once more bears the image of his Creator (cf. Col.
3.10; Eph. 4.24).[3]

3. HEILSGESCHICHTE.

In this sort of setting, Paul's *anthropology* assumes great
importance. There are some good Protestant monographs on
this subject.[4] But the discoveries at Qumran throw new light
on the subject. Thus the Pauline antithesis between σάρξ and

---

[1] G. Schrenk, *Urchristliche Missionspredigt im I. Jahrhundert*, in *Studien
zu Paulus*, Zurich, 1954, 131-148; *Der Römerbrief als Missionsdokument*,
op. cit., 81-106; G. Bornkamm, *Das Ende des Gesetzes, Paulusstudien*, Munich,
1952, 9-33; B. Reicke, *Natürliche Theologie nach Paulus*, in *Svensk Exegetisk
Arsbok*, 22-23, 1958, 154-167; S. Schulz, *Die Anklage in Röm I, 18-32*,
in *Theol. Zeitschrift*. Bâle, 14, 1958, 161-173.

[2] Cf. M. Pohlenz, *op. cit.*; O. Kuss, *Die Heiden und die Werke des
Gesetzes (nach Röm 2, 14-16)*, in *Münchener Theol. Zeitschrift*, 5, 1954,
77-98 (bibliog.).

[3] S. Mc. Casland, *The 'Image of God' According to Paul*, JBL, 69, 1950,
85-100; F. W. Eltester, *Eikon im Neuen Testament*, in *Beihefte zur* ZNW,
23, Berlin, 1958 (bibliog.).

[4] W. Gutbrod, *Die paulinische Anthropologie*, Stuttgart, 1934; J. A. T.
Robinson, *The Body (Studies in Biblical Theology*, 5), London 1952;
W. D. Stacey, *The Pauline View of Man*, London, 1956.—Cf. (Catholic):
K. Th. Schäfer, *Der Mensch in paulinischer Auffassung* in *Das Bild vom
Menschen (Festschrift für F. Tillmann)*, Dusseldorf, 1934, 25-35; J. Schmid,
art. *Anthropologie, Biblisch*, in *Lexikon für Theologie und Kirche 2*, vol. I,
Freiburg in Br., 1957, 611-614.

πνεῦμα,[1] and the 'dualistic' concept of man (Rom. 7),[2] which used often to be explained in terms of hellenistic influences, seem to have been perfectly acclimatized in late Judaism.[3] Paul makes use of Jewish assumptions :[4] this is shown by his thought, *heilsgeschichtlich* in character, of which we find a remarkable expression in the *Adam-Christ typology* which is basic to his entire soteriology (cf. Rom. 5.12-21; 1 Cor. 15.20-22, 45-49).[5] Catholic exegetes have been studying Paul's teaching on original sin afresh, and have successfully brought it into

---

[1] 'Flesh' and 'spirit'.

[2] W. SCHAUF, *Sarx* (*Neutest, Abh.*, XI, 1-2), Munster-in-W., 1924; W. G. KÜMMEL, *Römer 7 und die Bekehrung des Paulus*, Leipzig 1929; ID., *Das Bild des Menschen im Neuen Testament*, Zurich, 1948; C. H. LINDIJER, *Het begrip Sarx bij Paulus*, Assen, 1952; O. KUSS, *Römerbrief*, 507-440.

[3] K. G. KUHN, πειρασμός - ἁμαρτία - σάρξ im Neuen Testament und die damit zusammenhängenden Vorstellungen, in *Zeitschrift für Theologie und Kirche*, 49, 1952, 200-222; D. FLUSSER, *The Dualism of 'Flesh and Spirit' in the Dead Sea Scrolls and the New Testament*, in *Tarbiz*, 27, 1957-1958, 158-165; a different view is expressed in E. SCHWEIZER, *Die hellenistische Komponente im neutest.* σάρξ-*Begriff*. ZNW, 48, 1957, 237-253; R. E. MURPHY, *Bšr in the Qumrân literature and Sarks in the Epistle to the Romans*, in *Sacra Pagina*, II, Gembloux, 1959, 60-76.

[4] Another example: The idea of 'mystery', about which discussion is raging, also seems to have Jewish roots, cf. R. E. BROWN, *The Pre-Christian Semitic Concept of Mystery*, in CBQ, 20, 1958, 417-443; *The Semitic Background of the New Testament Mysterion*, Bib, 39, 1958, 426-448; 40, 1959, 70-87; B. RIGAUX, *Révélation des mystères et perfection à Qumrân et dans le Nouveau Testament*, NTS, 4, 1958, 237-262; J. COPPENS, *Le 'Mystère' dans la théologie paulinienne et ses parallèles Qumrâniens*, in *Littérature et théologie pauliniennes* (*Recherches bibliques*, 5), Paris, 1960, 142-165.

[5] A. VITTI, *Christus Adam*, Bib., 7, 1926; K. BARTH, *Christus-Adam nach Röm 5* (*Theol. Studien* 34), Zollikon-Zurich, 1952; M. BLACK, *The Pauline Doctrine of the Second Adam*, in *Scottish Journal of Theology*, 7, 1954, 170-179; S. LYONNET, *Quaestiones in Ep. ad Romanos*, I, Rome 1955, 182-243 (bibliog.); ID., in *Bib.*, 36, 1955, 436-456; in *Recherches de Science Relig.*, 44, 1956, 63-84; F. G. LAFONT, *Sur l'interprétation de Rom 5. 15-21*, art. cit. 45, 1957, 481-513; O. KUSS, *Römerbrief*, 224-275; R. BULTMANN, *Adam und Christus nach Röm 5*, ZNW, 50, 1959, 145-165.

focus.[1] But this antithesis between the two heads of mankind opens up still further horizons : it governs the sombre description of the ills of man until the coming of Christ; the conception of a divine plan leading sin to its climax of power (Rom. 7.13) before granting man, in Christ, a super-abounding salvation (Rom. 5.20); and the theme of the profound solidarity of believers and baptized with Christ (cf. our exposition of baptism and the Body of Christ below)—Christ who, as head of redeemed mankind, and the 'first-born of the dead' leads us to a bodily resurrection (1 Cor. 15.20-22) and reproduces in us the image of his glorious body (1 Cor. 15.49; cf. Rom. 8.29; Phil. 3.21). In this light, Paul's doctrine of the Resurrection,[2] the crowning point of his soteriology, becomes much more comprehensible.

It is also by reference to the *heilsgeschichtlich* character of Paul's thought,[3] that we can make some attempt at unravelling the Apostle's complicated statements about the *Law,* and

---

[1] Cf. A.-M. Dubarle, *Le péché originel dans les suggestions de l'Évangile,* in *Revue des Sciences Philos. et Théolog.,* 39, 1955, 603-614; Id., *Le péché originel dans saint Paul, ibidem,* 40, 1956, 213-254; Id., *Le Péché originel dans l'Écriture,* Paris 1958; J. Mehlmann, *Natura Filii irae (Ep. 2. 3),* Rome, 1957; J. de Fraine, *Adam et son lignage,* Bruges, 1959; L. Ligier, '*In quo omnes peccaverunt*', in *Nouv. Revue Théologique,* 92, 1960, 337-348; S. Lyonnet, *Le péché originel en Rom. 5. 12,* in Bib., 41, 1960, 325-355.

[2] H. Molitor, *Die Auferstehung der Christen und Nichtchristen nach dem Apostel Paulus (Neutest. Abh.,* XVI, I), Munster-in-W., 1933; L. Cerfaux, *La résurrection des morts dans la vie et la pensée de saint Paul,* in *Lumière et Vie,* I, 1952, 61-82; O. Cullmann, *Unsterblichkeit der Seele und Auferstehung der Toten* in *Theol. Zeitschrift* (Bâle), 12, 1956, 126-156; (on this point) Ch. Masson, *Immortalité de l'âme ou résurrection des morts?* in *Revue de Théol. et de Philos.,* 8, 1958, 250-267.

[3] In addition to Chapter IV, p. 57 n. 2: J. Munck, *Paulus und die Heilsgeschichte,* Copenhagen, 1954 (English translation 1959); G. Schrenk, *Die Geschichtsanschauung des Paulus,* in *Studien zu Paulus,* Zurich, 1954, 49-80; O. Kuss, *Der Römerbrief,* Excursus: *Die Heilsgeschichte,* 275-291.

display in its clarity the great theme of the 'Law and the Gospel'. A great deal of work has been done in this field, notably in the form of an interchange of views between the different confessions.[1] Paul seems to disparage the Law strongly, seeing its role in salvation-history as to intervene and intrude so that transgression might abound (Rom. 5.20a, cf. Gal. 3.19), and to reject it as incapable of giving life (Gal. 3.21). But it is equally certain that Paul also speaks of a Law of a completely different order—a 'Law of the Spirit' (Rom. 8.2)[2] a 'Law of Christ' (Gal. 6.2; cf. 1 Cor. 9.21), whose concrete realization lies in charity.

4. JUSTIFICATION AND FAITH

This brings us to a hotly disputed question—Paul's teaching on justification.[3] The controversy between the 'juridical' and

---

[1] P. BLÄSER, Das Gesetz bei Paulus (Neutest. Abh., XIX, 1-2), Munster-in-W., 1941; P. BENOIT, La loi et la croix d'après saint Paul, RB, 47, 1938, 481-509; W. GUTBROD, art. νόμος, TW, IV, 1061-1070 (bibliog.); CH. MAURER, Die Gesetzeslehre des Paulus, Zollikon-Zurich, 1941; CH. DE BEUS, Paulus Apostel der Vrijheid, Amsterdam, (1953); E. KAMLAH, Buchstabe und Geist, in Evangelische Theologie, 14, 1954, 276-282; W. JOEST, Gesetz und Freiheit 2, Gottingen, 1956; G. SÖHNGEN, Gesetz und Evangelium, Fribourg-Munich, 1957; P. BLÄSER, Gesetz und Evangelium, Catholica, 14, 1960, 1-23.

[2] S. LYONNET, Liberté chrétienne et loi nouvelle selon saint Paul, Rome, 1954; C. H. DODD, Ἔννομος Χριστοῦ, in Arcana revelata (Mélanges W. F. Grosheide), Kampen, 1951, 89-103.

[3] E. TOBAC, Le problème de la justification dans saint Paul (Diss. Lov.), Louvain, 1908 (=Gembloux, 1941); L. CERFAUX, art. Justice, Justification, DBS, IV, 1417-1496 (bibliography by A. DESCAMPS 1510); H. W. HEIDLAND, Die Anrechnung des Glaubens zur Gerechtigkeit, Stuttgart 1936; H. D. Wendland, Die Mitte der paulinischen Botschaft, Gottingen, 1935; S. DJUKANOVIC, Heiligkeit und Heiligung bei Paulus, Novi Sad, 1939; H. HOFER, Die Rechtfertigungsverkündigung des Paulus nach der neueren Forschung, Gutersloh, 1940; S. LYONNET, De 'Justitia Dei' in Epistola ad

'mystical' (or sacramental) concepts has lost its edge, for today it is recognized that Paul unites the two (compare Rom. 3-5 with 6-8).[1] However, some Protestants still support 'imputed' or 'forensic' justification:[2] this problem is tied up with the Lutherans' *simul justus et peccator*—a formula on which there is still no agreement.[3] On the other hand, we can now see more clearly that the Pauline polemic against the justice of works— the works of the Law through which man hopes to obtain justice and glory by virtue of his observance—is not incompatible with the epistle of St James, who demands that faith should not be left without 'works': that is, that it should not be divorced from the moral effort which it should naturally produce (James 2.14-26); we are better able to understand that Paul and James are looking at things from two different points of view, and are appealing to two different

---

Romanos, in *Verbum Domini*, 25, 1947 passim; ID., *Quaestiones in Ep ad Rom.*, I, 109-181; ID., in Bib, 38, 1957, 40-61; J. GIBLET, *De theologia justitiae Dei apud S. Paulum*, in *Collectanea Mechlin.*, 39, 1954, 50-55; G. H. W. LAMPE (and others), *The Doctrine of Justification by Faith*, London, 1955; C. HAUFE, *Die sittliche Rechtfertigungslehre des Paulus*, Halle, 1957; O. KUSS, *Römerbrief*, Excursus: *Die Gerechtigkeit Gottes* 115-131; S. LYONNET, *Justification, jugement, rédemption, principalement dans l'épître aux Romains*, in *Littérature et théologie pauliniennes* (*Recherches bibliques*, 5), Paris, 1960, 166-184.

[1] Cf. WEINEL, *Theologie*, 236-251; A. SCHWEITZER, *Mystik*, 201-221; the opposite view is expressed in W. GRUNDMANN, *Gesetz, Rechtfertigung und Mystik bei Paulus*, ZNW, 32, 1933, 52-65; A. OEPKE, in TW, I, 539; G. SCHRENK, art. cit., II, 212; cf. A. OEPKE, in *Theol. Literaturzeitung*, 77, 1952, 454-457; as also R. BULTMANN *Theol.*, 272-275.

[2] Cf. E. STAUFFER, *Theologie*, 121-123; the opposite view is expressed in E. J. GOODSPEED, *Justification*, JBL, 73, 1954, 86-91.

[3] Cf. R. GROSCHE, *Simul justus et peccator*, in *Pilgernde Kirche*, Freiburg in Br., 1938, 147-158; A. KIRCHGÄSSNER, *op. cit.* (Chapter II, p. 44 n. 5); P. BLÄSER, *Rechtfertigungsglaube bei Luther*, Munster-in-W., 1953; (Protestant) W. JOEST, *Paulus und das lutherische Simul Justus et Peccator*, in *Kerygma und Dogma*, I, 1955, 269-320.

suppositions.[1] Catholics admit that the expression *sola fide* is Pauline;[2] but this does not imply that there is any genuine agreement on the process of justification, and the way in which man realizes his salvation is still a matter of controversy. The exegete must now change his views on whether there existed in Judaism the idea of a justice, springing from God, and running counter to all observance of the Law, since this is clearly attested in the Qumran texts;[3] it is still a matter for debate, however, whether or not Paul was justified in his controversy with the Jews.[4]

There has been a similar rapprochement on Paul's conception of *faith*,[5] in the sense that Protestants no longer insist on the pure *fides fiducialis*, while Catholics emphasize the role of grace in the πίστις.[6] However, all the differences have not been resolved, and they are still very much in evidence on the question of the relationship between faith and baptism,[7] and of the

---

[1] B. BARTHMANN, *St. Paulus und St. Jakobus über die Rechtfertigung*, Freiburg in Br., 1897; (Protestants) G. EICHHOLZ, *Jakobus und Paulus*, Zollikon-Zurich, 1953; J. JEREMIAS, *Paul and James*, in *Expository Times*, 66, 1954-1955, 368-371; E. LOHSE, *Glaube und Werke. Zur Theologie des Jakobusbriefes*, ZNW, 48, 1957, 1-22.

[2] Cf. H. KÜNG, *Rechtfertigung*, Einsiedeln, 1957, 243-256; O. KUSS, *Römerbrief*, 134.

[3] S. SCHULZ, *Zur Rechtfertigung aus Gnaden in Qumran und bei Paulus*, in *Zeitschrift für Theologie und Kirche*, 56, 1959, 155-185.

[4] Cf. J. SCHOEPS, *Paulus*, 224-230; (on this point) F. MUSSNER in Bz, 4, 1960, 307-310.

[5] E. WISSMANN, *Das Verhältnis von* πίστις *und Christusfrömmigkeit bei Paulus* (*Forschungen zur Religion und literatur des Alten und Neuen Testaments*, 40), Gottingen, 1926; W. MUNDLE, *Der Glaubensbegriff des Paulus*, Leipzig, 1932; R. BULTMANN, in TW, VI, 218-224 (Bibl. p. 175). On the Catholic side, P. ANTOINE, in DBS, III, 296-302; O. KUSS, *Römerbrief*, Excursus: *Der Glaube*, 131-154.

[6] 'Faith'.

[7] Cf. J. DUPLACY, *Le salut par la foi et le baptême d'après le Nouveau Testament*, in *Lumière et Vie*, 27, 1956, 3-52.

general meaning of baptism.[1] Lively controversy on the conception of baptism in Paul and in the early Church[2] was roused among Protestants, notably by K. Barth's work : 'Baptism of adults or children?'[3] Catholic exegesis also took a hand in the positive study of the Pauline texts on baptism (especially Rom. 6.1-14), thus provoking in turn a controversy among Catholics. The point at issue concerns the essential meaning of baptism as a 'death and resurrection with Christ'; more precisely, scholars ask whether this has to be understood in terms of the theology of the mysteries, as O. Casel understood it,[4] or in terms of other categories (solidarity with the new Adam, 'communion with the death and life of Christ, etc.)[5]'. This controversy, conducted with a keen sense of the problem, and still very much alive, has at least allowed us to clarify and

[1] Among a host of works, cf. J. COPPENS, Art. *Baptême*, DBS, I, 852-924; O. CULLMANN, *Die Tauflehre des Neuen Testaments*, Zurich, 1948 (English translation 1951); W. F. FLEMINGTON, *The New Testament Doctrine of Baptism*, London, 1948; F. J. LEENHARDT, *Le baptême chrétien, son origine, sa signification*, Neuchâtel-Paris, 1946; R. SCHNACKENBURG, *Das Heilsgeschehen bei der Taufe nach dem Apostel Paulus (Münchener Theol. Studien,* I, 1), Munich, 1950; J. SCHNEIDER, *Die Taufe im Neuen Testament,* Stuttgart, 1952; *Lumière et Vie,* 26-27, 1956; J. CREHAN, *Ten Years' Work on Baptism and Confirmation,* in *Theological Studies,* 17, 1956, 494-515.

[2] Cf. H. SCHLIER, *Zur kirchlichen Lehre von der Taufe,* in *Theol. Literaturzeitung,* 72, 1947, 321-336; J. SCHNEIDER, *op. cit.;* J. JEREMIAS, *Die Kindertaufe in den ersten vier Jahrhunderten,* Gottingen, 1958 (bibliog.) (English translation 1960); K. ALAND, *Die Säulingstaufe im Neuen Testament und in der alten Kirche,* Munich, 1961.

[3] K. BARTH, *Die Kirchliche Lehre von der Taufe,* Zollikon-Zurich, 1943 (English translation 1954).

[4] V. WARNACH, *Taufe und Christusgeschehen nach Römer 6,* in *Archiv für Liturgiewissenschaft,* 3, 1954, 284-366 (bibliog.); ID., *Die Tauflehre des Römerbriefes in der neueren theologischen Diskussion,* art. cit., 5, 1958, 274-332 (bibliog.); cf. O. KUSS, *Römerbrief,* 307-319.

[5] R. SCHNACKENBURG, *op. cit.;* ID., *Todes und Lebensgemeinschaft mit Christus. Neue Studien zu Röm 6, 1-11,* in *Münchener Theol. Zeitschrift,* 6, 1955, 32-53 (bibliog.); (with references to E. DRUWE, A. GRAIL, M. FRAYEMAN, E. STOMMEL, etc.); cf. on this point D. MOLLAT, in *Recherches de Science Relig.,* 45, 1957, 240-245.

penetrate more deeply into the thought of St Paul, and it was fruitful also for theology in general.[1]

5. CHRISTOLOGICAL MYSTICISM

The formulas in σύν (Χριστῷ) [2] which we come across in the context of baptism, lead to the formulas ἐν Χριστῷ [4] and bring us to an area of Pauline research in which a great deal of work has been done in recent years: christological mysticism. This expression is itself a matter for debate for, ever since the time (twenty years ago) when A. Deissmann and others[5] published their 'mystical' interpretation of Paul, scepticism on the subject of Pauline mysticism has been growing.[6] Leaving aside the

[1] On the theology of the mysteries, see also B. NEUNHEUSER, in *Archiv für Liturgiewissenschaft*, III, 2, 1954, 104-122; *art. cit.*, III, 1956, 316-324; ID., *Mysteriengegenwart, Das Anliegen Dom Casels und die neueste Forschung*, in *Studia Patristica*, II, (*Texte und Untersuchungen*, 67), Berlin, 1957, 54-63; J. GROTZ, *Das Gegenwärtige Gespräch über die Mysterientheologie* (a review of published work), in *Geist und Leben*, 28, 1955, 381-386; P. WEGENAER, *Heilsgegenwart. Das Heilswerk Christi und die Virtus Divina in den Sakramenten*, Munster-en-W., 1958.

[2] 'With (Christ)'.

[3] E. LOHMEYER, Σὺν Χριστῷ, in *Festgabe für A. Deissmann*, Tubingen, 1927, 218-257; R. SCHNACKENBURG, *Das Heilsgeschehen*, 167-175; J. DUPONT, Σὺν Χριστῷ. *L'union avec le Christ suivant saint Paul*, I, Bruges-Louvain-Paris, 1952; G. OTTO, *Die mit syn verbundenen Formulierungen im paulinischen Schrifttum* (a manuscript dissertation), Berlin, 1952; P. BONNARD, *Mourir et vivre avec Jésus-Christ selon saint Paul*, in *Revue d'histoire et de philos. relig.*, 36, 1956, 101-112; O. KUSS, *Römerbrief*, Excursus: '*Mit Christus*', 329-381; B. M. AHERN, *The Fellowship of his Sufferings*, CBQ, 22, 1960, 1-32.

[4] 'In Christ'.

[5] A. DEISSMANN, *Die neutestamentliche Formel 'in Christo Jesu'*, Marbourg, 1892; ID., *Paulus*, Tubingen, 1925. Recent works are listed in A. WIKENHAUSER, *Die Christusmystik des Apostels Paulus 2*, Freiburg in Br., 1956 (English translation 1960).

[6] Cf. K. DEISSNER, *Paulus und die Mystik seiner Zeit 2*, Leipzig, 1921; H. E. WEBER, '*Eschatologie*' und '*Mystik*' im Neuen Testament, Gutersloh, 1930; M. DIBELIUS, *Glaube und Mystik bei Paulus*, in *Botschaft und Geschichte, Gesammelte Aufsätze*, II, Tubingen, 1956, 94-116; ID., *Paulus und die Mystik, art. cit.*, 134-159.

question of the term itself (and it is an ambiguous one) we can say that what we have to do is to reach a theological understanding of the profound 'union' with Christ which this and other formulas denote. The interpretation suggested by A. Wikenhauser is both extremely lucid and prudent[1] but, in spite of this, all the problems have not yet been solved. The possible meanings of the frequently used formula ἐν Χριστῷ have been the object of fresh philological discussions,[2] and how it is to be interpreted theologically raises even more problems. Above all it is necessary, even for Catholics, to define more precisely Paul's conception of the divine πνεῦμα, which is of such importance for throwing light on the union of believers with their glorious Saviour.[3] For while it may be true that for Paul the *Holy Spirit* is not solely the third divine person, it is likewise true that neither does he think of him (as Deissmann thought) as an 'atmosphere' or a fluid, but as linked to the

---

[1] *Op. cit.*, (p. 83 n. 5 above); see also J. HUBY, *Mystiques paulinienne et johannique*, Paris, 1946; W. GROSSOUW, *In Christ*, Westminster, Maryland, 1952.

[2] Cf. F. BÜCHSEL, '*In Christus*' *bei Paulus*, ZNW, 42, 1949, 141-158; F. NEUGEBAUER, *Das paulinische*, ἐν Χριστῷ NTS, 4, 1957-1958, 124-138; H. L. PARISIUS, *Über die forensische Deutungsmöglichkeit des paulinischen* ἐν Χριστῷ, ZNW, 49, 1958, 285-288; J. A. ALLAN, *The 'in Christ' formula in Ephesians*, NTS, 5, 1958-1959, 54-62.

[3] H. BERTRAMS, *Das Wesen des Geistes nach der Anschauung des Paulus* (*Neutest. Abh.* IV, 4), Munster-in-W., 1913; W. REINHARD, *Das Wirken des Hl. Geistes im Menschen nach den Briefen des Apostels Paulus*, Freiburg in Br., 1918; P. GÄCHTER, *Zum Pneumabegriff des hl. Paulus*, in *Zeitschrift für Kath. Theologie* 53, 1929, 345-408; E. FUCHS, *Christus und der Geist bei Paulus*, Leipzig, 1932; H. D. WENDLAND, *Das Wirken des Hl. Geistes in den Gläubigen nach Paulus*, in *Theol. Literaturzeitung*, 77, 1952, 457-470; E. SCHWEIZER, art. πνεῦμα TW, VI, 413-436 (there is a full bibliography, 330-333); N. Q. HAMILTON, *The Holy Spirit and Eschatology in Paul*, Edinburgh, 1957; O. KUSS, *Römerbrief* 540-545; E. BEST, *One Body in Christ, A Study in the Relationship of the Church to Christ in the Epistles of the Apostle Paul*, London, 1955.

risen and living Lord (cf. 1 Cor. 15.45; 2 Cor. 3.17).[1] But this
is only one of the points from which we must advance.[2] Many
scholars think also that the ἐν Χριστῷ must be understood
first of all in an ecclesiological sense, that is as ἐν τῷ σώματι
τοῦ Χριστοῦ[3], and this leads us to the problems of the
'Body of Christ' (see below). The formulas assume peculiar
originality and depth when Paul comes to speak of his
sufferings, which he bears in close union with Christ (2 Cor.
4.10f.; 13.4; Phil. 3.10f., etc.) and which he takes upon himself for others, for the Church (2 Cor. 1.5f.; 4.15; Col. 1.24).[4]

Paul's somatology (his conception of the σῶμα τοῦ Χριστοῦ)[5]
is the object of lively controversy,[6] and this fact is important

---

[1] Cf. K. Prümm, *Israels Kehr zum Geist,* in *Zeitschrift für Kath. Theologie,*
72, 1950, 385-442; B. Schneider *'Dominus autem Spiritus est'* (2 Co
3. 17 s.), Rome, 1951 (on this, see P. Benoit, in RB, 59, 1952, 129-131;
L. Cerfaux, in *Ephemerides Theol. Lovanienses,* 1954, 477 f.).

[2] Cf. also S. Zedda, *L'adozione a figlio di Dio e lo Spirito Santo,* Rome,
1952 (on this, see P. Benoit, in RB, 61, 1954, 142-144); P. Bläser,
'Lebendigmachender Geist', in *Sacra Pagina,* II, Gembloux, 1959, 404-413;
I. Hermann, *Kyrios und Pneuma. Studien zur Christologie der paulinischen
Hauptbriefe (Studien zum Alten und Neuen Testament,* 2), Munich, 1961,
(bibliog.).

[3] 'In the body of Christ'.

[4] J. Kremer, *Was an den Leiden Christi noch mangelt* (on Col. 1, 24b)
(Diss. Greg.) (Bonner Bibl. Beiträge), Bonn, 1956; M. Schmid, *Die
Leidensaussage in Kol 1. 24* (manuscript dissertation), Vienna, 1956;
G. le Grelle, *La plénitude de la parole dans la pauvreté de la chair d'après
Col 1. 24,* in *Nouvelle Revue Théol.,* 91, 1959, 232-250.

[5] 'The body of Christ'.

[6] Among the many studies, we might cite: E. Mersch, *Le corps
mystique du Christ 2,* 2 vols., Paris-Brussels, 1936 (English translation
reprinted 1956); A. Wikenhauser, *Die Kirche als der mystische Leib
Christi nach dem Apostel Paulus 2,* Munster-in-W., 1940; E. Percy, *Der
Leib Christi in den paulinischen Homologumena und Antilegomena,* Lund, 1942;
S. Hanson, *The Unity of the Church in the New Testament,* Uppsala, 1946;
L. S. Thornton, *The Common Life in the Body of Christ 2,* Westminster,
1944; W. Goossens, *L'Église, Corps du Christ,* Paris, 1949; L. Malevez,
L'Église, Corps du Christ, in *Recherches de sciences Relig.,* 32, 1944, 27-94;
J. A. T. Robinson, *The Body,* London, 1952; A. Oepke, *Leib Christi oder
Volk Gottes bei Paulus?,* in *Theol. Literaturzeitung,* 79, 1954, 363-368;
E. Best, *One Body in Christ,* London, 1955; H. Schlier, *Corpus Christi,*

for ecclesiology.[1] The attempts made to explain[2] or at least to throw a little light upon[3] his conception of the Body of Christ, starting from gnostic mythology, deserve attention in the case of the letters from captivity, although here too, contradictory voices are not lacking.[4] In 1 Corinthians and Romans, his conception is a little different (Paul does not distinguish head and body, but body and members), and seems to depend on the image of an organism. For this reason, independently of the question of the origin of the expression, many exegetes interpret the body of Christ in a very literal manner, as the body of the glorified person of Christ;[5] to express the relationship between this 'collective' body and the Christ who is in heaven, L. Cerfaux speaks of a 'mystical identification'—an idea which it is not easy to define theologically.[6] Similarly, there is dispute over

in *Reallexikon für Antike und Christentum*, vol. 3, Stuttgart, 1957, 334-453 (bibliog.); P. BONNARD, *L'Église Corps du Christ dans le paulinisme*, in *Revue de Théologie et de Philosophie*, 8, 1958, 268-282; G. MARTELET, *Le mystère du corps et de l'Ésprit dans le Christ ressuscité et dans l'Église*, in *Verbum Caro*, 12, 1958,31-33. P. POKORNY, Σῶμα Χριστοῦ *im Epheserbrief*, in *Evang. Theologie*, 20, 1960, 456-464; C. COLPE, *Zur Leib-Christi-Vorstellung im Epheserbrief*, in *Judentum, Urchristentum, Kirche (Festschrift für J. Jeremias)*, Berlin, 1960, 172-187.

[1] L. CERFAUX, *La Théologie de l'Église suivant saint Paul 2*, Paris, 1948 (English translation 1959); L. S. THORNTON, *Christ and the Church*, London, 1956; A. NYGREN, *L'unité de l'Église*, in *Revue d'Histoire et de Philos. Relig.*, 37, 1957, 283-293; H. SCHLIER, *Die Einheit der Kirche*, in *Die Zeit der Kirche, Gesammelte Aufsätze*, Freiburg in Br., 1956, 287-299.

[2] Cf. E. KÄSEMANN, *Leib und Leib Christi*, Tubingen, 1933; R. BULTMANN, *Theologie*, 178 f.

[3] H. SCHLIER, *Der Brief an die Epheser*, Dusseldorf, 1957, *passim*, and the excursus, p. 90-96.

[4] F. MUSSNER, *Christus, das All und die Kirche, Studien zur Theologie des Epheserbriefes*, Trèves, 1955; C. COLPE, *art. cit.*

[5] E. PERCY, *loc. cit.*; P. BENOIT, *Corps, Tête et Plérôme dans les épîtres de la captivité*, RB, 63, 1956, 5-44; J. REUSS, *Die Kirche als 'Leib Christi' und die Herkunft dieser Vorstellung bei dem Apostel Paulus*, BZ, 2, 1958, 103-127.

[6] L. CERFAUX, *La Théologie de l'Église*, 206 f.; the opposite view is presented in T. ZAPELENA, *Vos estis corpus Christi (1 Co 12, 27)*, in *Verbum Domini*, 37, 1959, 78-95, 162-170; cf. J. HAVET, *La doctrine paulinienne du 'Corps du Christ'. Essai de mise en point*, in *Littérature et théologie paulinienne (Recherches bibliques, 5)*, Paris, 1960, 185-216.

the importance of the sacraments for the constitution (baptism) and the unity (eucharist)[1] of the 'body of Christ', for there is no agreed exegesis of 1 Cor. 12.13 and 10.16 f. Moreover, we must bear in mind Paul's other images and viewpoints (the people of God) on the subject of the Church: his ecclesiology is a rich one.

6. THE PAULINE ETHIC

As far as the Pauline ethic is concerned,[2] we must note that it is a characteristic trait of his to juxtapose the indicative (or soteriological) and the imperative (that is, the properly paren-thetical) forms of the same assertion; the tension thus created between the certainty of salvation and the fear of not being saved (for the Christian is himself still awaiting the judgement (2 Cor. 5.10))[3] is unmistakable.[4] This special characteristic of Christian existence cannot be understood except in the context

[1] P. NEUENZEIT, Das Herrenmal. Studien zur paulinischen Eucharistie Auffassung (Studien zum Alten und Neuen Testament, 1), Munich, 1960.

[2] K. BENZ, Die Ethik des Apostels Paulus (Bibl. Studien, XVII, 3-4), Freiburg in Br., 1912; A. JUNCKER, Die Ethik des Apostels Paulus, Halle, 2 vols., 1904-1919; M. S. ENSLIN, The Ethics of Paul, Cambridge, 1930; F. V. FILSON, St Paul's Conception of Recompense, Leipzig, 1931; M. E. ANDREWS, The Ethical Teaching of Paul, Baltimore, 1934; B. REICKE, The N.T. Conception of Reward in Aux Sources de la Tradition chrétienne (Mélanges M.Goguel), Paris, 1950, 145-206; C. SPICQ, Vie morale et Trinité sainte selon saint Paul (Lectio Divina, 19), Paris, 1957; G. DIDIER, Désintéressement du Chrétien. La rétribution dans la morale de saint Paul (Théologie, 32), Paris, 1955. Further references in Chapter VIII, section 4.

[3] Cf. H. BRAUN, Gerichtsgedanke und Rechtfertigungslehre bei Paulus, Leipzig, 1930; F. V. FILSON, St. Paul's Conception of Recompense, Leipzig, 1931; D. MOLLAT, Art. Jugement, DBS, IV, 1362-1374.

[4] Cf. W. MUNDLE, Religion und Sittlichkeit bei Paulus in ihrem inneren Zusammenhang, in Zeitschrift für systemat. Theologie, 4, 1926-1927, 456-482; H. D. WENDLAND, Ethik und Eschatologie in der Theologie des Paulus, in Neue kirchl. Zietschr., 41, 1930, 757-783, 793-811; R. SCHNACKENBURG, Das Heilsgeschehen, 189-195; A. KIRCHGÄSSNER, op. cit., 147-157; E. MOCSY, Problema imperativi ethici in justificatione paulina, in Verbum Domini,

of the eschatological situation, 'between the times', between the inauguration and the consummation of salvation. Hence we can speak of three successive moments: Christ's death has delivered us from this present age (Gal. 1.4), and we are now united to Christ by an 'existential' link, but the return of Christ is something for which we still hope (1 Cor. 10.11; Rom. 13. 11-14). Thus, the Christian's position in relation to this world is defined (1 Cor. 7.29-31; Rom. 12.2); however, God's salvific action, already realized by Christ, is still the major theme of Paul's parenesis.[1] There are a number of special questions, and several concepts and themes of his ethic and parenesis, which are still awaiting more detailed study.[2]

7. ESCHATOLOGY

Finally, a host of problems lie hidden in Paul's eschatology. The most important is the need to arrive at a proper understanding of his expectation of an imminent Parousia (and we

---

25, 1947, 204-217, 264-269; E. DINKLER, *Zum Problem der Ethik bei Paulus: Rechtsnahme und Rechtsverzicht (1 Cor. 6, 1-11)*, in *Zeitschrift für Theologie und Kirche*, 49, 1952, 167-200; H. H. REX, *Das ethische Problem in der eschatologischen Existenz bei Paulus* (a manuscript dissertation), Tubingen, 1954, cf. *Theol. Literaturzeitung*, 80, 1955, 250 f.; H. M. SCHENKE, *Das Verhältnis von Indikativ und Imperativ bei Paulus* (a manuscript dissertation), Berlin, 1957.

[1] L. NIEDER, *Die Motive der Religiös-sittlichen Paränese in den paulinischen Gemeindebriefen (Münchener Theol. Studien,* I, 12), Munich, 1956; a different view is expressed in G. STAFFELBACH, *Die Vereinigung mit Christus als Prinzip der Moral bei Paulus,* Freiburg in Br., 1932; M. E. ANDREWS, *The Problem of Motive in the Ethics of Paul,* in *Journal of Religion,* 13, 1933, 200-215.

[2] Cf. J. KOOP, *De paraenese van den Apostel Paulus,* Zalt-Bommel, 1926; A. VÖGTLE, *Die Tugend-und Lasterkataloge im Neuen Testament, (Neutest. Abh.,* XVI, 4-5), Munster-in-W., 1936; L. BOUVET, *L'ascèse dans saint Paul* (Thesis), Lyons, 1936; M. HANSEN, *Het ascetisme en Paulus' verkondiging van het nieuwe leven (Diss.),* Zutphen, 1938.

cannot reasonably deny that he does expect this).[1] Paul does not look upon this as a dogma, for he also accepted the prospect of death to be anticipated and of an 'intermediary state' between death and resurrection (2 Cor. 5.1-10).[2] The most important thing in his eyes is to belong to the Lord (2 Cor. 5.8) and to be always near him, whether at the Parousia (1 Thess. 4.17), or after death (Phil. 1.23). It is certainly impossible to mistake the explicit, 'futuristic' nature of his expectations (parousia, resurrection, judgement)—despite certain obscurities.[3] Moreover we are not able to interpret these existentially, as if they were merely the expression of man's 'selbstverständnis', liberated from himself by the grace of God, and continually renewing his commitment to God;[4] but it is just as important not to reduce Paul's real 'eschatological' attitude to what he says in 1 Thess. 5.1-11. On this point, it is difficult to find a penetrating and positive study which we could set in the balance against the existentialist theologians.

[1] F. Tillmann, *Die Wiederkunft Christi nach den paulinischen Briefen* (*Bibl. Studien*, XIV, 1-2), Freiburg in Br., 1909; F. Guntermann, *Die Eschatologie des hl. Paulus* (*Neutest. Abh.*, XIII, 4-5), Munster-in-W. 1952; B. Rigaux, *Saint Paul. Les épîtres aux Thessaloniciens* (*Études bibliques*), Paris-Gembloux, 1956, 195-280 (bibliog.).

[2] E.-B. Allo, *Saint Paul. Seconde épître aux Corinthiens 2* (*Études bibliques*), Paris, 1956, Excursus, 137-155; 155-160; J. N. Sevenster, *Einige Bemerkungen über den 'Zwischenzustand' bei Paulus*, NTS, 1, 1954-1955, 291-296; A. Feuillet, *La demeure céleste et la destinée des chrétiens*, in *Recherches de Science Relig.*, 44, 1956, 161-192; 360-402.

[3] On Antichrist, see B. Rigaux, *L'Antéchrist*, Gembloux-Paris, 1932; Id., *Thessaloniciens*, 259-280 (bibl.); on the resurrection, see H. Molitor, *op. cit.*, (p. 78 n. 2 above); O. Cullmann, *op. cit.*, (p. 78 n. 2 above); J. Schniewind, *Die Leugner der Auferstehung in Korinth, Nachgelassene Reden und Aufsätze*, Berlin, 1952, 110-139; W. Pfendsack, *Auferstehung der Toten. Eine Auslegung von I Kor 15*, Bâle, 1953; W. Schmithals, *Die Gnosis in Korinth* (*Forsch. zur Relig. und Lit. des Alten und Neuen Test.*, 66), Gottingen, 1956.

[4] R. Bultmann, *Geschichte und Eschatologie* (Chapter IV, p. 57 n. 2); the opposite view is expressed in B. Rigaux, *Thess.*, 213-222.

CHAPTER VI

THE THEOLOGY OF ST JOHN

1. GENERAL QUESTIONS: JUDAISM OR HELLENISM?

IT IS EVEN MORE important with John than with Paul to begin by identifying the original context and religious background of his theology.[1] Was it already separated from Judeo-Palestinian thought, or did its roots lie therein? What label can we give it: Judeo-Hellenistic, gnostic, or qumranian—for the parallels with the Dead Sea Scrolls are, to say the least, impressive? The author of the fourth Gospel (and of John's epistles, if we are to attribute these to the same author) does not strike one with the individuality and spontaneity of St Paul, although a work of this kind is inexplicable except when seen as the work of a

[1] An outline of the bibliography: W. F. HOWARD, *The Fourth Gospel in Recent Criticism and Interpretation*, revised by C. K. BARRETT, London, 1955; P.-H. MENOUD, *L'évangile de Jean d'après les recherches récentes 2*, Neuchâtel-Paris, 1947; ID., *Les études johanniques de Bultmann à Barrett*, in *L'Évangile de Jean (Recherches bibliques, III)*, Louvain, 1958, 11-40; J. BEHM, *Der gegenwärtige Stand der Erforschung des Johannesevangeliums*, in *Theol. Literaturzeitung*, 73, 1948, 21-30; E. HAENCHEN, *Aus der Literatur zum Johannesevangelium*, 1929-1956, in *Theol. Rundschau*, 23, 1955, 295-335; D. M. STANLEY, *Bulletin, Theological Studies*, 17, 1956, 516-531; F.-M. BRAUN, *Où en est l'étude du 4e Évangile?*, in *Ephem. Theol. Lovan.*, 32, 1956, 535-546; R. SCHNACKENBURG, *Neuere englische Literatur zum Johannesevangelium*, BZ, 2, 1958, 144-154.

strong personality:[1] and it is therefore particularly important to identify his spiritual environment.[2] However, it is more difficult to solve this problem with John than with Paul's epistles: it is possible to discover close kinship with several different centres of thought—with Rabbinical Judaism, Hellenistic Judaism (Philo), hermeticism—that 'superior religion of Hellenism'—gnosticism and mandeism, as has been shown by C. H. Dodd, in his great work on the fourth Gospel,[3] and F. M. Braun, in some noteworthy studies.[4] A great deal, too, has already been written on the relationship between Qumran and John's Gospel.[5] One thing, however, is certain: it would

---

[1] We differ from A. KRAGERUD, *op. cit.* (Chapter III, p. 53 n. 3) cf. C. K. BARRETT, *The Gospel according to St John*, London, 1955, 83-119; F.-M. BRAUN, *Jean le Théologien et son Évangile dans l'Église ancienne (Études bibliques)*, Paris, 1959.

[2] Among earlier works, cf. A. SCHLATTER, *Sprache und Heimat des vierten Evangelisten*, Gutersloh, 1902; F. BÜCHSEL, *Johannes und der hellenistische Synkretismus*, Gutersloh, 1928; the mandean 'gnostic' theory has been defended ever since R. BULTMANN, *Die Bedeutung der neuerschlossenen mandäischen und manichäischen Quellen für das Verständnis des Johannesevangeliums*, ZNW, 24, 1925, 100-146, especially in the commentaries by W. BAUER, *Das Johannesevangelium 3 (Handbuch zum Neuen Testament, 6)*, Tubingen, 1933; R. BULTMANN, *Das Evangelium des Johannes 4 (H. A. W. MEYER, 2nd. part)*, Gottingen, 1953, with a complementary fascicule in 1957; on the new sources (Qumran), cf. notes 4 and 5 below.

[3] C. H. DODD, *The Interpretation of the Fourth Gospel*, Cambridge, 1953; on this subject, see among others: P. WINTER, in *Theol. Literaturzeitung*, 80, 1955, 141-150; D. MOLLAT, in *Recherches de Science Relig.*, 44, 1956, 422-442.

[4] F.-M. BRAUN, *Essénisme et Hermétisme*, in *Revue Thomiste*, 54, 1954, 523-558; *Hermétisme et Johannisme*, ibidem, 55, 1955, 22-42, 259-299; *L'arrière-fond judaïque du quatrième évangile et la communauté de l'Alliance*, RB, 62, 1955, 5-44; *Le Mandéisme et la secte essénienne de Qumrân (Orient. et Bibl. Lovan., 1)*, Louvain, 1957; *L'arrière-fond du quatrième évangile (Recherches bibliques, III)*, Louvain, 1958, 179-196; *L'Évangile de saint Jean et les grandes traditions d'Israel*, in *Revue Thomiste*, 59, 1959, 421-450; 60, 1960, 165-184, 325-363.

[5] In addition to F.-M. BRAUN (see the previous note), cf. L. MOWRY, *The Dead Sea Scrolls and the Background for the Gospel of St. John*, in *Biblical*

be false and premature to reduce Johannine theology to any single one of the spiritual currents that we have mentioned; it would seem that this theology, just as much as Pauline theology, is original, and specifically Christian.[1]

2. THE SON OF GOD

Leaving aside the sections in the manuals which deal with this subject, no general exposition of John's theology has appeared. It is true that several good outlines of John's thought[2] exist, but these are hardly more than introductions. We might even wonder at the fact that christology—the central issue of John's teaching—has for a long time[3] had no scholar ready to deal

---

Archaeologist, 17, 1954, 78-94; J. SCHMITT, *Les écrits du Nouveau Testament et les textes de Qumran*, in *Revue de Sciences Relig.*, 29, 1955, 381-401; 39, 1956, 55-74; 261-282; O. CULLMANN, *The Significance of the Qumran Texts for Research into Beginnings of Christianity*, JBL, 74, 1955, 213-226; R. E. BROWN, *The Qumran-Scrolls and the Johannine Gospel and Epistles*, CBQ, 17, 1955, 403-419, 559-574; W. F. ALBRIGHT, *Recent Discoveries in Palestine and the Gospel of St. John*, in *In Honour of C. H. Dodd*, 1956, 153-171; K. SCHAEDEL, *Das Johannesevangelium und die Kinder des Lichts* (Dissertation), Vienna, 1952; G. BAUMBACH, *Qumran und das Johannes-Evangelium*, Berlin, 1957 (parts have been published).

[1] Cf. P.-H. MENOUD, *L'originalité de la pensée johannique*, in *Revue de Théologie et de Philosophie*, 1940, 233-261; E. SCHWEIZER, *Orthodox Proclamation*, in *Interpretation*, 8, 1954, 387-403; see also the following notes.

[2] W. VON LOEWENICH, *Johanneisches Denken*, in *Theologische Blätter*, 15, 1936, 260-275; W. F. HOWARD, *Christianity according to St. John*, London, 1943; W. GROSSOUW, *Pour mieux comprendre saint Jean*, Bruges, 1946 (English translation London, 1958); W. STÄHLIN, *Das johanneische Denken*, Witten, 1954; E. K. LEE, *The Religious Thought of St. John*, London, 1950.

[3] W. LÜTGERT, *Die Johanneische Christologie 2*, Gutersloh, 1916. For recent works, cf. J. SCHNEIDER, *Die Christusschau des Johannesevangeliums*, Berlin, 1935; E. GAUGLER, *Das Christuszeugnis des Johannesevangeliums*, in *Jesus Christus im Zeugnis der Heiligen Schrift und der Kirche*, Munich, 1936, 34-67; J. E. DAVEY, *The Jesus of St. John*, London, 1958; J. GIBLET,

with it. We are grateful to J. Dupont for his fine Essays,[1] but they do not exhaust the subject, and are too exclusively interested in the Old Testament background. By the time we come to John, we have to recognize the fact that New Testament christology has reached the end of an evolutionary process, from which Hellenistic influences cannot be wholly excluded. This is notoriously true for the concept of *Logos* which, although not central to John's theology, is still of fundamental importance, as we can see particularly from its relationship to the incarnation theme.[2] G. Kittel[3] had already tried to reduce this theme to biblical antecedents, and had drawn attention to a primitive, synoptic theology of the 'Word of God'. But J. Starcky was right to say that the use of *Logos* without a complement 'is more in conformity with Hellenistic usage than with biblical style'[4] and that, during his long stay in Ephesus, John cannot have remained cut off from Hellenistic thought.[5] Of course, he does also see a close relationship with the speculations of Hellenistic Judaism on wisdom,[6] but thinks that it was on his own initiative and quite deliberately that John substituted

---

Jésus et le 'Père' dans le Quatrième Évangile (*Recherches bibliques*, III), Louvain, 1958, 111-130.

[1] J. Dupont, *Essais sur la christologie de saint Jean*, Bruges, 1951.

[2] For works on the Logos, we should turn, above all, to: J.-M. Voste, *De Prologo Johanneo et Logo*, Rome, 1928; G. Kittel, Art. λέγω etc., in TW, IV, 130-140 (bibliog. 70 f.); A. J. Surjansky, *De mysterio Verbi incarnati ad mentem B. Johannis Apostoli*, I, Rome, 1941; J. Dupont, *op. cit.* (previous note) 11-58; J. Starcky, art. *Logos*, DBS, V, 486-496 (bibliog.); C. H. Dodd, *Interpretation*, 263-285; O. Moe, *Logosbegrepet i Johannesevangeliets sammenhang*, in *Svensk Exegetisk Arsbok*, 22-23, 1957-1958, 111-118.

[3] *Op. cit.*, (previous note).

[4] *Op. cit.*, 486.

[5] *Op. cit.*, 491.

[6] Cf. especially C. Spicq, *Le Siracide et la structure littéraire de saint Jean*, in *Mémorial M.-J. Lagrange*, Paris, 1940, 183-195; J. Dupont, *op. cit.*; M.-E. Boismard, *Le Prologue de saint Jean*, Paris, 1953 (English translation 1957).

Logos for the term *Wisdom*. As far as the 'creative and revelative' function of the *Logos* is concerned, he brings forward certain parallel texts from Philo and hermetic literature,[1] but shows that John gave a Christian interpretation to these ideas.[2] And if we take the specifically Christian character of the redemptive function of the *Logos* into account, we can leave out of consideration the gnostic texts (which are late, in any case), in which the *Logos* appears as a revealer and redeemer.[3]

The *Logos* theme is an example of how John reveals that, while his roots were always in the Old Testament, he was also open to Hellenistic Judaism and to the spiritual currents of his time; but we must be careful not to reduce everything to this sort of pattern. When we turn to the central title 'Son of God', and to 'Son' used in an absolute sense, (unfortunately, this is a subject on which we do not possess any recent Catholic monographs),[4] we have to point to several hints in the Synoptics which John might have deepened. The same is true of the title 'Son of Man' : the formulas peculiar to John are to be explained by the revelation of Jesus, by the way it was interpreted in the early Church and by John's own interpretation, taken all

---

[1] *Op. cit.*, 493.

[2] *Op. cit.*, 494.

[3] R. BULTMANN, *Der religionsgeschichtliche Hintergrund des Prologs zum Johannes-Evangelium*, ΕΥΧΑΡΙΣΤΗΡΙΟΝ (*Mélanges H. Gunkel*), 2nd part, Gottingen, 1923, 1-26; ID., *Das Evangelium des Johannes;* W. BAUER, *Das Johannesevangelium*, 6-10; H. H. SCHAEDER, *Der 'Mensch' im Prolog des IV. Evangeliums*, in Reitzenstein-Schaeder, *Studien zum antiken Synkretismus aus Iran und Griechenland*, Leipzig-Berlin, 1926, 306-341.

[4] See the 'Hellenistic' reduction by G. P. WETTER, *Der Sohn Gottes* (*Forschungen zur Religion und Literatur des Alten und Neuen Testaments*, 26), Gottingen, 1916; R. BULTMANN, *Theologie*, 379-396; S. SCHULZ, *Untersuchungen zur Menschensohn-Christologie im Johannesevangelium*, Gottingen, 1957, 124-142, etc. The opposite viewpoint is put forward in O. CULLMANN, *Christologie*, 276-313.

together; the influence of earlier pronouncements on the title 'Son of Man'—those found in Jewish apocalyptic writing—is still doubtful, in spite of S. Schulz' remarkable piece of research.[1]

3. THE DISCOURSES ON REVELATION

Recent research has paid special attention to the style of Jesus' *discourses on revelation* in John. The mere fact of such a public revelation—even though it was, in some sense, limited to believers alone—is surprising enough in itself,[2] and even more surprising is the formula 'Εγώ εἰμι..., which we meet with so frequently. In spite of E. Schweitzer's penetrating work,[3] the influence of gnostic, and particularly of mandaean, vocabulary is not certain; according to more recent research,[4] the presence of the formula in the theophanies and the words spoken by God in the Old Testament provides a better explanation, at least from the theological point of view. While it is the case that we still need to study the style of the discourses—a style which recurs in several passages of John's first epistle—

---

[1] *Op. cit.*, (previous note) (with a very full bibliography).

[2] H. H. HUBER, *Der Begriff der Offenbarung im Johannes-Evangelium*, Gottingen, 1934; H. SCHULTE, *Der Begriff der Offenbarung im Neuen Testament*, Munich, 1949 (bibliog.); cf. O. BETZ, *Offenbarung und Schriftforschung in der Qumransekte* (*Wissenschaftl. Untersuchungen zum N.T.*, 6), *Tubingen*, 1960.

[3] E. SCHWEIZER, *Ego eimi . . . Die religionsgeschichtliche Herkunft der johanneischen Bildreden* (*Forschungen zur Religion und Literatur des Alten und Neuen Testaments*, 56), Gottingen, 1939.

[4] J. BRINKTRINE, *Die Selbstaussage Jesu* 'Εγώ εἰμι, in *Theologie und Glaube*, 47, 1957, 34-36; E. STAUFFER, *Probleme der Priestertradition*, in *Theol. Literaturzeitung*, 81, 1956, 135-150, especially 147 f.; ID., *Jesus, Gestalt und Geschichte* (*Dalp-Taschenbücher*, 332), Berne, 1957, 130-146; H. ZIMMERMANN, *Das absolute ἐγώ εἰμι als die neutestamentliche Offenbarungsformel* (Catholic dissertation), Bonn, BZ, 4, 1960, 54-69, 266-276.

and to define its *Sitz im Leben*,[1] it is quite certain that we must reject the hypothesis of a discourse on revelation in the gnostic style as its special source.[2] Perhaps this special source was a prophetic or pneumatic discourse, for which a circle of prophet-missionaries of the early Church were responsible?[3] This is a purely arbitrary suggestion.

4. THE SPIRIT

A detailed examination still remains to be done of John's conception of the *Spirit*.[4] The words he uses with reference to the Paraclete[5] were already a part of the 'settled tradition', but they fit well into John's spiritual world. The Spirit is not presented as he from whom prophetic and ecstatic gifts originate; he is the principle of life (cf. Jn. 3.5-8; 6.63; 7. 38f.), and more

---

[1] Cf. W. NAUCK, *Die Tradition und der Charakter des ersten Johannesbriefes* (*Wissensch. Untersuchungen zum Neuen Testament*, 3), Tubingen, 1957.

[2] R. BULTMANN, *Das Evangelium des Johannes*, passim; H. BECKER, *Die Reden des Johannesevangeliums und der Stil der gnostischen Offenbarungsrede* (*Forschungen zur Religion und Literatur des Alten und Neuen Testaments*, 68), Gottingen, 1956; the opposite viewpoint is presented in S. SCHULZ, *Komposition und Herkunft der Johanneischen Reden*, Stuttgart, 1960 (bibliog.).

[3] A. KRAGERUD, *op. cit.*

[4] H. WINDISCH, *Jesus und der Geist im Johannesevangelium*, in *Amicitiae Corolla, Festschrift für J. Rendel Harris*, London, 1933, 303-318; W. F. HOWARD, *Christianity* (see p. 92 n. 2 above), 71-80; C. K. BARRETT, *The Holy Spirit in the Fourth Gospel*, in *Journal of Theological Studies*, 51, 1950, 1-15; R. SCHNACKENBURG, *Die Johannesbriefe*, 187-191; K. WENNEMER, *Geist und Leben bei Johannes*, in *Geist und Leben*, 30, 1957, 185-198; G. SCHULZE-KADELBACH, *Zur Pneumatologie des Johannesevangeliums*, ZNW, 46, 1955, 297 f.; J. COPPENS, *Le don de l'Ésprit d'après les textes de Qumran et le quatrième Évangile*, in *Recherches bibliques*, III, Louvain, 1958, 209-223; D. E. HOLWERDA, *The Holy Spirit and Eschatology in the Gospel of John*, Kampen, 1959.

[5] Earlier works are examined in P.-H. MENOUD, *L'Évangile de Jean* (see p.90 n.1 above), 57-60; on this subject, W. MICHAELIS, *Zur Herkunft des johanneischen Paraklet-Titels*, in *Coniectanea Neotest.*, XI, *Mélanges A. Fridrichsen*, Lund-Copenhagen, 1947, 147-162; G. BORNKAMM, *Der*

than this, he serves Jesus' revelation in his role as Witness and Interpreter (14.26; 15.26; 16.13f.).

5. THE DOCTRINE OF SALVATION

The Holy Spirit, whom the glorified Christ sends from the Father (16.7), continues and perfects Jesus' *work of salvation*. John's soteriology has its own distinctive characteristics; it is marked by dualism[1]—of the two worlds, higher and lower, of life and death, of light and darkness,[2] and of truth[3] (in its existentialist sense) and falsehood. The *career of the Redeemer* leads him from the divine, heavenly sphere to a perishable world, which is earthly and separated from God; this is in order to restore the divine life to men and to raise them with

Paraklet im Johannesevangelium, Festschrift R. Bultmann, Stuttgart, 1949, 12-35; R. BULTMANN, *Das Evangelium des Johannes*, 437-440; M. F. BERROUARD, *Le Paraclet, défenseur du Christ devant la conscience du croyant (Jn. 16, 8-11)*, in *Revue des Sciences Philos. et Théol.*, 33, 1949, 361-389; J. G. DAVIES, *The Primary Meaning of παράκλητος*, in *Journal of Theological Studies*, 4, 1953, 35-38; J. BEHM, art. παράκλητος, TW, V, 798-812.

[1] Cf. E. PERCY, *Untersuchungen über den Ursprung der johanneischen Theologie*, Lund, 1939; K. G. KUHN, *Die Sektenschrift und die iranische Religion*, in *Zeitschrift für Theologie und Kirche*, 49, 1952, 296-316; K. SCHAEDEL, *op. cit.* (cf. p.91 n.5 above); G. BAUMBACH, *op. cit.*; H.-J. SCHOEPS, *Urgemeinde, Judenchristentum, Gnosis*, Tubingen, 1956; F. NÖTSCHER, *Zur theologischen Terminologie der Qumran-Texte (Bonner Bibl. Beiträge*, 10), Bonn, 1956, 79-133; K. SCHUBERT, *Die Gemeinde vom Toten Meer*, Munich-Bâle, 1958 (English translation, 1959); R. SCHNACKENBURG, art. *Dualismus*, in *Lexikon für Theologie und Kirche 2*, vol. 3, Freiburg in Br., 1959, 583-585. Cf. H. W. HUPPENBAUER, *Der Mensch zwischen zwei Welten*, Zurich, 1959 (Qumran).

[2] S. AALEN, *Die Begriffe 'Licht' und 'Finsternis' im Alten Testament, im Spätjudentum und im Rabbinismus*, Oslo, 1951.

[3] F. NÖTSCHER, *'Wahrheit' als theologischer Terminus in den Qumran-Texten*, in *Festschrift für V. Christian*, Vienna, 1956, 83-92; J. LOZANO, *El concepto de verdad en San Juan* (manuscript dissertation), Munich, 1959; I. DE LA POTTERIE, *L'arrière-fond du thème johannique de vérité*, in *Studia Evangelica (Texte und Untersuchungen*, 73), Berlin, 1959, 277-294.

himself to the heavenly glory. The two high points in this career
are presented with incomparable style, allowing no possibility
of misunderstanding—that is, no gnostic interpretation : the
Incarnation, the act by which the divine Word himself assumed
a mortal σάρξ,[1] and the Cross, which paradoxically becomes
an 'elevation' and a 'glorification'.[2] John insists with equal
firmness on the efficacy of these saving events : an efficacy
which is universal and extends to the whole of mankind (cf.
3.16; 4.42; 6.33, 51, etc.). There is still no completely satis-
factory exposition of this magnificent vision, contrasted with
the gnostic myth of redemption and the hypothesis of its pre-
tended influence on John's theology.

6. FAITH

The one thing expressly demanded of man is *faith;* this is the
great Johannine formula for salvation : 'He who believes in the
Son has eternal life' (Jn. 3.16, 36, etc.).[3] Life (eternal life)
becomes the central concept, the definition of present and
future salvation; on this question we now have a good

[1] S. DE AUSEJO, *El concepto de 'carne' aplicado a Cristo en el IV Evangelio,*
in *Estudios biblicos,* 17, 1958, 411-427; *Sacra Pagina,* II, Gembloux, 1959,
219-234.
[2] A. VERGOTE, *L'exaltation du Christ en croix selon le quatrième Évangile*
(*Analecta Lovan. Bibl. et Orient.,* II, 29), Bruges-Paris, 1952; W.
GROUSSOUW, *La glorification du Christ dans le quatrième Évangile* (*Recherches
Bibliques,* III), Louvain, 1958, 131-145; W. THÜSING, *Die Erhöhung und
Verherrlichung Jesu im Johannesevangelium* (*Neutest. Abh.* XXI, 1-2),
Munster-en-W., 1960.
[3] There is a bibliography in TW, VI, 174 f.; R. BULTMANN, *op. cit.,*
224-230 on John; in addition, see F.-M. BRAUN, *L'accueil de la foi selon
saint Jean,* in *La Vie Spirituelle,* 92, 1955, 344-363; M. BONNINGUES, *La
foi dans l'Évangile de saint Jean,* Paris, 1955; F. ROUSTANG, *Les moments de
l'acte de foi et ses conditions de possibilité* (on Jn. 4) in *Recherches de Science
Relig.,* 46, 1958, 344-378; A. DECOURTRAY, *La conception johannique de la
foi,* in *Nouvelle Revue Théol.,* 91, 1959, 561-576.

monograph by F. Mussner.[1] The power and attraction of
Johannine theology springs precisely from these captivating and
extremely rich formulas; today, as much as ever, they possess
a great capacity for radiating light on the religious level, but
they still have not had the benefit of a sufficiently positive exposition. However, we do possess excellent studies on light,[2]
glory,[3] joy,[4] divine sonship[5] and truth.[6] On charity, both as the
sole motive force for God's salvific action, and as man's
reply, in partnership with faith, we now possess a literature
about which we have every reason to be happy.[7]

---

[1] F. MUSSNER, ΖΩΗ. Die Anschauung vom 'Leben' im vierten Evangelium,
(Münchener Theol. Studien, II, 5), Munich, 1952, (bibliog.); in addition,
see: J. DUPONT, Essais, 109-232; W. TURNER, Believing and Everlasting
Life, in Expository Times, 64, 1952-1953, 50-52.

[2] See the bibliography in J. DUPONT, Essais, 61 f.; on this subject,
see J. DUPONT, op. cit., 61-105; B. BUSSMANN, Der Begriff des Lichtes beim
Hl. Johannes, Munster-en-W., 1957.

[3] See the bibliography in J. DUPONT, Essais, 236, and R. SCHNACKEN-
BURG, art. Doxa, in Lexikon für Theologie und Kirche 2, Freiburg-in-Br.,
1959, 533 f.; T. CRISAN, De notione Doxa in Evangelio S. Joannis in luce
Veteris Testamenti (Diss.), Rome, 1953.

[4] E. G. GULIN, Die Freude im Neuen Testament, II, Das Johannesevangelium,
Helsinki, 1936.

[5] W. TWISSELMANN, Die Gotteskindschaft der Christen nach dem Neuen
Testament (Diss.), Gutersloh, 1940; W. SCHWEITZER, Gotteskindschaft,
Wiedergeburt und Erneuerung im Neuen Testament und in seiner Umwelt
(Diss.), Tubingen, 1944; F. BÜCHSEL, art. γεννάω, TW, I, 669-671;
J. HUBY, Mystiques (Chapter V, p. 84 n. 1), 155-170; R. SCHNACKENBURG,
Johannesbriefe, 155-162.

[6] See p. 97 n. 3 above.

[7] W. LUTGERT, Die Liebe im Neuen Testament, Leipzig, 1905; J. MOFFAT,
Love in the New Testament, London, 1929; A. NYGREN, Eros und Agape,
2 vols., Gutersloh, 1930-7 (2nd ed. 1956) (English translation 1953);
V. WARNACH, op. cit. (Chapter I, p. 23 n. 3); ID. Liebe, Bibeltheologisches
Wörterbuch, Graz-Vienna-Cologne, 1959, 502-542 (bibliog.); C. SPICQ,
op. cit. (Chapter II, p. 44 n. 1); ID., Notes d'exégèse johannique: La charité
est amour manifeste, RB, 65, 1958, 358-370; T. BAROSSE, The Relationship
of Love to Faith in St. John in Theological Studies, 18, 1957, 539-559;
L. MORALDI, Dio è Amore, Rome 1954; C. OGGIONI, La dottrina della
carità nel IV Vangelo e nella prima lettera di Giovanni, in Scrinium Theologi-
cum, 1, 1953, 221-293.

7. THE CHURCH

What place does the *Church* have in John's theology of salvation? The problem has only been posed quite recently,[1] for St John has been too long regarded as the recognized champion of individual salvation. And yet the presentation of the Church is more clear-cut in his theology than might at first sight appear. How does the Paraclete testify before the world, if not through the mouth of the Church (cf. Jn. 16.8-11)? Where are the 'children of God who are scattered abroad' (11.52) gathered together, if not in the flock of Christ, which includes, as well as believing Jews, those who 'are not of this fold' (10.16)? Think too of the sending of the disciples into the world (17.18; 20.21), of Christ's prayer for future believers (17.20f.), of the 'greater works' which he promised his disciples should perform (14.12), of the account of Jesus' stay in Samaria (chapter 4) with its significant formulas on the harvest (4.36-38), and of the account of the arrival of the 'Greeks' (12.20-23): all this betrays a lively and burning interest in missionary work.[2] And

---

[1] E. GAUGLER, *Die Bedeutung der Kirche in den johanneischen Schriften*, in *Internationale kirchliche Zeitschrift*, 14, 1924, 97-117; 181-219; 15, 1925, 27-42; D. FAULHABER, *Das Johannesevangelium und die Kirche*, Heidelberg, 1935; E. L. ALLEN, *The Jewish-Christian Church in the Fourth Gospel*, JBL, 74, 1955, 88-92; A. CORELL, *Consummatum est. Eschatology and Church in the Gospel of St. John*, New York, 1959; E. SCHWEIZER, *Der Kirchenbegriff im Evangelium und den Briefen des Johannes*, in *Studia Evangelica* (*Texte und Untersuchungen*, 73), Berlin, 1959, 363-381.

[2] K. BORNHÄUSER, *Das Johannesevangelium eine Missionsschrift für Israel,* Gutersloh, 1928; the same approach is to be found in: W. C. VAN UNNIK, *The Purpose of St. John's Gospel*, in *Studia Evangelica* (*Texte und Untersuchungen*, 73), Berlin, 1959, 382-411; J. A. T. ROBINSON, *The Destination and Purpose of St. John's Gospel*, NTS, 6, 1960, 117-121; W. OEHLER, *Das Johannesevangelium eine Missionsschrift für die Welt*, Gutersloh, 1936; ID., *Zum Missionscharakter des Johannes-Evangeliums*, Gutersloh, 1941.—However, John's Gospel is primarily an 'intra-community' work, and is only indirectly aimed at the Mission. Cf. the following notes.

the examination of these texts might very well help us better to discover the milieu from which the Gospel originally sprang, as well as its background.[1]

8. WORSHIP AND THE SACRAMENTS

A vigorous and fruitful dialogue has developed on *worship* and the *sacraments* in John's Gospel. O. Cullmann provided the decisive impulse which started this discussion in his book *Early Christian Worship*,[2] where he presents the thesis that one of the major aims of the author of the fourth Gospel is to show the relationship between the worship of the early Church and the life of the historical Jesus. According to Cullmann, numerous pericopes have the sacraments of baptism and the eucharist as their background. The discussion which was thus begun[3] at least showed clearly that the sacraments play an important role in John's thought; with their roots in Jesus' expiatory death (cf. Jn. 19.34f.), they make Christ's salvific work present, and through the intermediary of the Holy Spirit, communicate its vivifying power to believers (cf. 1 Jn. 5.6-8).[4] In the light of this, it is possible to arrive at a better understanding of the discourse

---

[1] O. CULLMANN, *Samaria and the Origins of the Christian Mission*, in *The Early Church*, London, 1956, 185-192; ID., *L'opposition contre le Temple de Jérusalem, motif commun de la théologie johannique et du monde ambiant*, NTS, 5, 1958-1959, 157-173; P. GEOLTRAIN, *Esséniens et Hellénistes*, in *Theologische Zeitschrift* (Bâle), 15, 1959, 241-254.

[2] O. CULLMANN, *Urchristentum und Gottesdienst 2* (*Abhandlungen zur Theologie des Alten und Neuen Testaments*, 3), Zurich, 1950; French translation: *Les sacrements dans l'Évangile johannique*, Paris, 1951; English translation, *Early Christian Worship*, 1953.

[3] For the bibliography, cf. R. SCHNACKENBURG, *Die Sakramente im Johannesevangelium*, in *Sacra Pagina*, II, Gembloux, 1959, 235-254; P. NIEWALDA, *Sakramentssymbolik im Johannesevangelium?* Limburg, 1958.

[4] Cf. SCHNACKENBURG, art. cit.; H. SCHÜRMANN, *Die Eucharistie als Repräsentation und Applikation des Heilsgeschehens nach Joh. 6. 53-59*, in *Trierer Theol. Zeitschrift*, 68, 1959, 20-45, 108-118.

on the Bread of life (Jn. 6), especially of the way it is put together, and of its two levels of meaning : Jesus himself is the
living bread come down from heaven, which becomes euchar-
istic bread for believers.[1] Baptism, too, has new light thrown on
it, when we ask where the evangelist's interest lies in his account
of the washing of the feet (Jn. 13.6-10), and whether the baptismal parenesis is the concrete *Sitz im Leben* of 1 John.[2] In
like manner, research needs to be done on the (sacramental)
forgiveness of sins (cf. Jn. 20.22f.), for the epistle pays particular
attention to the problem of impeccability and sin in the life of
Christians.[3] A deeper study of John's view of *sin* is much to be
desired—sin as a power which separates man from God (the
unbelief of Jn. 16.9!), as eschatological malice (1 Jn. 3.4),[4]
and as a human weakness which unsettles Christians and is a
burden to the community.

9. SYMBOLISM

A healthy moderation ought to prevent us from pushing John's
symbolism too far.[5] But any exegesis which stopped at the
external facts and at the most obvious meaning of the words

---

[1] Cf. H. SCHÜRMANN, *Joh. 6, 51c—Ein Schlüssel zur grossen johanneischen Brotrede*, BZ, 2, 1958, 244-262; the article by the same author, quoted in the previous note, contains a detailed bibliography.

[2] W. NAUCK, *op. cit.*, (p. 96 n. 1 above).

[3] Cf. A. KIRCHGÄSSNER, *op. cit.* (Chapter II, p. 44 n. 5); S. LYONNET, *op. cit.* (Chapter II, p. 44 n. 5); R. SCHNACKENBURG, *Johannesbriefe*, 253-258 (bibliog.); M.-E. BOISMARD, *Jésus Sauveur d'après saint Jean*, in *Lumière et Vie*, 15, 1954, 105-110. (Eng. trans. reprinted London, 1962.)

[4] I. DE LA POTTERIE, *Le péché c'est l'iniquité (I Jn. 3, 1)*, in *Nouvelle Revue Théol.*, 78, 1956, 785-797.

[5] Cf. F. QUIÉVREUX, *Le structure symbolique de l'Évangile de saint Jean*, in *Revue d'Histoire et de Philosophie Relig.*, 33, 1953, 123-165; H. SAHLIN, *Zur Typologie des Johannesevangeliums*, Uppsala, 1950; M.-E. Boismard, *Du Baptême à Cana (Jn. 1. 19-2. 11)*, (*Lectio Divina*, 18), Paris, 1956; P. NIEWALDA, *op. cit.* (p. 101 n.3 above).

would fail to understand the theological profundity of the 'pneumatic' Gospel. The first part is a 'book of signs' and John's conception of the σημεῖα[1] reveals the deep christological and soteriological meaning of the great miracles, although without weakening their reality as carefully established facts. This double character is particularly apparent in the healing of the man born blind (chapter 9 : Jesus, the light of the world) and in the raising of Lazarus (chapter 11 : Jesus, the source of life). It is as if the mystery of the Incarnation were being continued in the works done by the Son of God on earth; his hidden glory is revealed by 'signs' to the eyes of believers (Jn. 1.14; 2.11; 11.40).[2] Not all of Jesus' actions have an equally obvious significance, but even the purification of the Temple and what was said about it[3] assume a theological meaning in John's eyes; the temple which Jesus will destroy and rebuild in three days is his body (2.21ff). In cases where John does not give us his own interpretation, for instance, the account of Cana, there is room for the hypotheses of exegetes.[4] In this particular episode, a further difficulty is raised—what is the meaning of Jesus' reply to his mother : a saying of some importance for us Catholics in

---

[1] 'Signs'.

[2] L. CERFAUX, Le Christ et ses miracles dans l'Évangile de saint Jean, in L'attente du Messie (Recherches bibliques, I), Louvain, 1954, 131-138; J. P. CHARLIER, La notion de signe (σημεῖον) dans le quatrième Évangile, in Revue des Sciences Philos. et Théol., 43, 1959, 434-448; D. MOLLAT, Le Sémeion johannique, in Sacra Pagina, II, Gembloux, 1959, 209-218.

[3] A.-M. DUBARLE, Le signe du Temple (Jn. 2. 19), RB, 48, 1939, 21-44; X. LEON-DUFOUR, Le signe du temple selon saint Jean, in Recherches de Science Relig., 39, 1951, 155-175; M. SIMON, Retour du Christ et reconstruction du Temple dans la pensée chrétienne primitive, in Aux sources de la tradition chrétienne, in Mélanges M. Goguel, Neuchâtel-Paris, 1950, 247-257; E. F. SCOTT, The Crisis in the Life of Jesus. The Cleansing of the Temple and its Significance, New York, 1952; M. SABBE, Tempelreiniging en Tempellogion, in Collationes Brugenses et Gandav., 2, 1956, 289-299; 466-480.

[4] Among numerous works on the subject, we might quote: K. L. SCHMIDT, Der johanneische Charakter der Erzählung vom Hochzeitswunder in Kana, in Harnack-Ehrung, 1921, 32-43; O. CULLMANN, Urchristentum und Gottesdienst, 67-72; R. SCHNACKENBURG, Das erste Wunder Jesu, Freiburg in

the field of mariology.[1] *Quot capita, tot sensus!* It is unlikely
that agreement can be reached—at least on the level of exegesis
and biblical theology—on how the evangelist conceived the role
of the mother of God in salvation-history (see also Jn. 19.26f.).[2]

10. UNION WITH CHRIST AND GOD

Whatever may be the mystical profundity of the texts in John
on *Union with Christ and God*[3]—formulas which present
characteristic differences from those in St Paul—we cannot
forget that John has a practical and positive manner of exhort-
ing us to the Christian life[4] (1 Jn!).

A deeper and more penetrating study of the parabolic discourse on the true vine and the branches abiding in Christ and
in his love (Jn. 15.1-10) is to be desired.

Br., 1951; H. VAN DEN BUSSCHE, *Het Wijnwonder te Cana*, in *Collationes
Gandavenses*, 2, 1952, 193-225; J. MICHL, *Die Hochzeit zu Kana, Kritik
einer Auslegung*, in *Theologie und Glaube*, 45, 1955, 334-348; CH. P.
CEROKE, *Jesus and Mary at Cana: Separation or Association?* in *Theological
Studies*, 17, 1956, 1-38.

[1] On Jn. 2.4, in addition to the previous note, see especially:
H. VAN DEN BUSSCHE, *De betekenis van het Uur in het vierde Evangelie*, in
Collationes Gandavenses, 2, 1952, 97-108; J. LEAL, *La hora de Jesús, la
hora de su Madra*, in *Estud. Eccles.*, 26, 1952, 147-168; J. MICHL, *Bemerkungen zu Jn 2.4*, Bib, 36, 1955, 492-509; CH. P. CEROKE, *The Problem
of Ambiguity in John 2.4*, CBQ, 21, 1959, 316-340 (bibliog.).

[2] Cf. F.-M. BRAUN, *La Mère des Fidèles*, Tournai-Paris, 1953; P.
GAECHTER, *Maria im Erdenleben 2*, Innsbruck-Vienna-Munich, 1954;
B. J. LE FROIS, *The Woman Clothed with the Sun (Ap 12). Individual or
Collective?*, Rome, 1954, (bibliog.); A. KASSING, *Die Kirche und Maria.
Ihr Verhaltnis im 12 Kap. der Apokalypse*, Dusseldorf, 1958; J. GALOT,
Marie dans l'Évangile, Paris-Louvain, 1958.

[3] Cf. J. HUBY, *Mystiques*, 145-216; R. SCHNACKENBURG, *Johannesbriefe*,
91-95; B. LAMMERS, *Die Menein-Formeln der Johannesbriefe* (Diss. Greg.),
Rome, 1954.

[4] F.-M. BRAUN, *Morale et Mystique à l'école de saint Jean*, in *Morale
chrétienne et requêtes contemporaines*, Tournai-Paris, 1954, 74-84; O. PRUNET,
La morale chrétienne d'après les écrits johanniques, Paris, 1957; SUITBERTUS
A. S. JOANNE A. CRUCE, *Die Vollkommenheitslehre des ersten Johannesbriefes*,
Bib., 39, 1958, 319-333; 449-470.

11. MORALITY

John's *morality* is a morality of charity—charity proving itself in action. John succeeds admirably in giving a unity to his morality, centring it on what was in fact the essential thing in Jesus' mind : anyone who has experienced God's love, and who claims to love God, must also love his brothers. This 'new commandment' which Jesus gave (Jn. 13.34; cf. 1 Jn. 2.7 ff.) is explained by the eschatological condition of salvation; it does not limit the scope of Jesus' demands to the circle of brothers in the faith, but it does point Christians to the field of action closest to hand.

12. ESCHATOLOGY

This brings us back to the *eschatological* question, which is particularly pressing in the case of John. Has he eliminated the future, 'dramatic' eschatology, in order to interpret it in terms of the present, in a purely 'existentialist' way?[1] Beyond doubt, the traditional concepts have a new ring to them here : the emphasis is on a salvation which has already been realized. But John also expects a future fulfilment; and the terms in which this is expressed cannot be separated from their context, as if they had been produced by some ecclesiastical editor, or, in the case of 1 Jn., by a completely different author.[2] Under the

---

[1]R. Bultmann, *Die Eschatologie des Johannes-Evangeliums,* in *Glauben und Verstehen, Gesammelte Aufsätze,* I, Tubingen, 1933, 134-152; Id,. *Evangelium des Johannes,* passim. The opposite viewpoint is expressed in G. Stählin, *Zum Problem der johanneischen Eschatologie,* ZNW, 33, 1934, 225-259; B. Aebert, *Die Eschatologie des Johannesevangeliums* (a Protestant dissertation at Breslau), Wurzburg, 1936; E. Gaugler, *op. cit.* (p. 92 n. 3 above), 57f.; W. F. Howard, *Christianity* (p. 92 n. 2), 106-128. Cf. the following note.

[2] Cf. C. K. Barrett, *The Place of Eschatology in the Fourth Gospel,* in *Expository Times,* 59, 1947-1948, 302-305; H. Blauert, *Die Bedeutung*

influence of forces which need to be examined more closely, John has shifted the emphasis, and truly 'interpreted' Jesus' eschatological message; but he has not falsified it, nor has he stunted it. He, too, teaches (in a way different from Paul, but in profound agreement with him) an attitude which is simultaneously an assured hope of a future consummation, and a certainty of already being loved by God and saved. It would be worth bringing into the full light of day all that in John's theology has permanent value and ever-increasing contemporary relevance.

der Zeit in der johanneischen Theologie (manuscript, Protestant dissertation), Tubingen, 1953; O. LINTON, *Johannesevangelist og eskatologien,* in *Svensk Exegetisk Arsbok,* 22-23, 1957-1958, 98-110; A. CORELL, *op. cit.* (p. 100 n. 1 above); D. E. HOLWERDA, *op. cit.* (p. 96 n. 4 above).

CHAPTER VII

THE THEOLOGY OF THE OTHER WORKS OF THE NEW TESTAMENT

I. THE PASTORAL EPISTLES

OLDER MANUALS GROUP THE epistles of controversial authenticity (the *antilegomena*), and the other works which have clearly been influenced by Paul, under the heading of 'deutero-Paulinism'. Although we shall not enter here into the controversy over the authenticity of the pastoral epistles, we can say that separate treatment of the three letters addressed to individuals does seem justified. They are important not only because we can study in them the way in which the organization and the ministers of the Church had developed; they also contain their own theology[1] and their own morality—both strongly tinged with Hellenism. Do they already witness to a retreat from the Pauline Gospel, and to a sliding towards a 'pre-Catholicism', which could no longer understand the loftiness and the purity of the primitive, eschatological, message?[2] Or do these epistles rather serve to throw more light on certain authentic aspects of the Pauline message? In Paul, as well, do we already find catalogues of virtues and vices, which are not simply Hellenistic

[1] W. NAUCK, *Theologie der Pastoralbriefe I* (manuscript dissertation), Gottingen, 1950. Cf. *Theol. Literaturzeitung*, 79, 1954, 124 f.
[2] This view is held particularly by R. BULTMANN, *Theologie*, 3rd part.

or pagan in structure, but which have numerous antecedents in a Judaism which did not shut itself off from the influence of Hellenism.[1] Of course, when we compare them with the other epistles we notice the appearance of new expressions like πιὲφάνεια,[2] or εὐσέβεια;[3] but this growing adoption of the Christian Kerygma to the Hellenistic world which it was conquering, and in which it was henceforward to find its audience, seems to us to be a completely legitimate and necessary process. This is *a fortiori* true of 2 Peter, which (because of 1.4) seems to hold more interest for dogmatic theologians than biblical scholars.[4]

2. THE EPISTLE TO THE HEBREWS

This epistle, which long remained in the background of interest, today wields an attraction for which we have cause to be grateful. Even Catholic scholars postulate someone other than Paul as the author, and this seems to be largely justified, in view of the theology it expresses; for this reason, there is increasing interest in its own particular spiritual milieu, which reminds us strongly of the mentality of Hellenistic Judaism such as we know it at Alexandria.[5] Theologians are not interested merely in a few isolated characteristics, such as the christology of the High

---

[1] A. VÖGTLE, *op. cit.* (Chapter V, p. 88 n. 2); S. WIBBING, *Die Tugend- und Lasterkataloge im Neuen Testament und ihre Traditionsgeschichte unter besonderer Berücksichtigung der Qumran-Texte* (*Beihefte zur ZNW*, 25), Berlin, 1959.

[2] E. PAX, *op. cit.* (Chapter II, p. 44 n. 7).

[3] W. FOERSTER, Εὐσέβεια *in den Pastoralbriefen*, NTS, 5, 1958-1959, 213-218.

[4] But see the good commentary by J. CHAINE, *Les Épîtres Catholiques* (*Études bibliques*), Paris, 1939.

[5] Cf. especially C. SPICQ, *L'épître aux Hébreux* (*Études bibliques*), I, Paris, 1952, 39-91 ('Philonism').

Priest,[1] the idea of sacrifice,[2] or the concept of perfection;[3] they are much more interested in its fundamental theological conception; for, in spite of its conclusion, this long work, although written in the epistolary style, has more of the atmosphere of a treatise or homily.[4] It long seemed indisputable that the author intended to demonstrate, by means of an allegorical and typological exegesis of Scripture and referring constantly to the Jewish liturgy as it was still being practised, the superiority of the High Priest of the New Testament, and of his unique sacrifice, over the Jewish ritual of sacrifice.[5] But after E. Käsemann's impressive study[6]—which is a little too much orientated

---

[1] G. Schille, *Erwägungen zur Hohepriesterlehre des Hebräerbriefes*, ZNW, 46, 1955, 81-109; H. Nakagawa, *Christology in the Epistle of the Hebrews* (Dissertation), Yale University, 1955; Teodorico da Castel San Pietro, *Il sacerdotio celeste di Cristo nella lettera agli Ebrei*, in *Gregorianum*, 39, 1958, 319-334; O. Cullmann, *Christologie*, 82-107.

[2] W. von Loewenich, *Zum Verständnis des Opfergedankens im Hebräerbrief*, in *Theologische Blätter*, 12, 1933, 167-172; A. Vanhoye, *De 'aspectu' oblationis Christi secundum Epistolam ad Hebraeos*, in *Verbum Domini*, 37, 1959, 32-38. Cf. also p. 111 n. 1 below.

[3] O. Michel, *Die Lehre von der christlichen Vollkommenheit nach der Anschauung des Hebräerbriefes*, in *Theologische Studien und Kritiken*, 106, 1934-1936, 333-355; F. Torm, *Om τελειοῦν i Hebr.* in *Svensk Exegetisk Arsbok*, 5, 1940, 116-125; E. Käsemann, *Das wandernde Gottesvolk. Eine Untersuchung zum Hebr.*, Gottingen, 1939 (=2, 1957), 82-90; P. J. du Plessis, ΤΕΛΕΙΟΣ, *The Idea of Perfection in the New Testament*, Kampen, 1959.

[4] Cf. the recent commentaries, which are numerous and of high quality; they are listed in A. Wickenhauser, *Einleitung*, 324 and 425. The work itself is called λόγος παρακλήσεως (Heb. 13. 22).

[5] This view is still expressed in C. Spicq, *Hébr.* I, 220-252: in his opinion, this 'treatise' was addressed to Jewish priests who had become Christians, perhaps at Caesarea in Palestine or at Antioch in Syria; for the opposite viewpoint, see F. Lo Bue, *The Historical Background of the Epistle to the Hebrews*, JBL, 75, 1956, 52-57 (Apollo is writing to a Judeo-Christian group in Corinth); H. Kosmala, *Hebräer-Essener-Christen*, Leyde, 1959 (he is writing to Essenes who have not yet been converted to the Christian faith). Now cf. C. Spicq, art. cit. below (p. 111 n. 2).

[6] *Op. cit.* (note 3 above).

towards 'gnosticism'—the Jesuit F. J. Schierse[1] also put forward a new thesis. In his view, this epistle was written from
within the community it addresses; the author intends to show
a community whose faith is faltering how, following the footsteps and in the company of their leader Jesus Christ, they
must climb the path which leads out of this earthly world
which is subject to decay to the heavenly world and the eschatological fulfilment. In addition, the author is inspired by liturgical ideas and formulas of which a sufficient explanation can
be found in the Septuagint—the heavenly sanctuary, the high
priest, and the perpetual sacrifice. For its *Sitz im Leben,* we
must turn to Christian worship, and then we will see the work
as a liturgical sermon, which still reflects the structure of the
divine service (196-209). This particularly stimulating study,
which neglects none of the theological themes nor the more
specific ideas of the epistle—those, that is, which reveal the
influence of Plato and Philo—has certainly provoked criticism;[2]
but, nevertheless, it does provide us with a guiding thread which
enables us for the first time to follow an otherwise baffling
string of ideas. The thesis was probably pushed too far; an
immediately liturgical *Sitz im Leben* is difficult to prove. But
we do concur in the essential conclusion—that the intention of
the author of Hebrews, as well as to interpret Jesus' death as a
sacerdotal act,[3] was to describe the passage of the people of God
on their journey (Heb. 3-4), with their leader Jesus Christ,
towards the promised land, and to inculcate the duties which
are part and parcel of this condition. However this may be,

---

[1] F. J. SCHIERSE, *Verheissung und Heilsvollendung. Zur theologischen Grundfrage des Hebräerbriefes (Münchener Theol. Studien,* I, 9), Munich 1955.

[2] O. KUSS, *Zur Deutung des Hebräerbriefes,* in *Theologische Revue,* 53, 1957, 247-254.

[3] O. KUSS, *Der theologische Grundgedanke des Hebräerbriefes. Zur Deutung des Todes Jesu im Neuen Testament,* in *Münchener Theol. Zeitschrift,* 7, 1956, 233-271.

theological research[1] must keep in its programme the hermeneutic and theological problem posed by this text, which, further-
more, has numerous links with other late works, and in particular with the Johannine writings.[2]

3. THE FIRST EPISTLE OF PETER

This fine letter, so full of riches, which comes to us from the
Christian Dispersion, has also recently been extensively studied,
as a good many substantial commentaries already demonstrate.[3] Here again, we are faced with the question of the
concrete 'Sitz im Leben' of its ideas and exhortations, which
reflect the influence of Pauline theology. It is not difficult here
to recognize allusions to baptism and to the state of persecution.

---

[1] A few of the works listed are difficult to find: R. A. MARTIN, *The
Exegetical Method of the Author of the Epistle to the Hebrews* (Diss.),
Princeton, 1952; A. B. MICHELSON, *Methods of Interpretation in the
Epistle to the Hebrews* (Diss.), Chicago, 1951; R. S. ECCLES, *Hellenistic
Mysticism in the Epistle to the Hebrews*, (Diss., Yale University), New
Haven, 1952. On the structure of the epistle to the Hebrews, cf. R.
GYLLENBERG, *Die Komposition des Hebräerbriefes*, in *Svensk Exegetisk
Arsbok*, 22-23, 1958, 137-147; A. VANHOYE, *La structure centrale de
l'Épître aux Hébreux* (8. 1-9, 28), in *Recherches de Science Relig.*, 47, 1959,
44-60.

[2] Cf. C. SPICQ, *Hébreux*, I, 109-138 (on John); 139-144 (on 1 Pet.);
ID., *L'épître aux Hébreux, Apollos, Jean-Baptiste, les Héllénistes et Qumrân*,
in *Revue de Qumrân*, 1, 1958-1959, 365-390;—for the links with Lucan
writings, cf. C. P. M. JONES, *The Epistle to the Hebrews and the Lucan
Writings*, in *Studies in the Gospels in Memory of R. H. Lightfoot*, ed. by
D. E. NINEHAM, Oxford, 1955, 113-143. Cf. also O. CULLMANN,
L'opposition . . . (Chapter VI, p. 101 n. 1).

[3] E. G. SELWYN, *The first epistle of St. Peter 2*, London, 1947; F. BEARE,
The First Epistle of Peter, Oxford, 1948; C. E. CRANFIELD, *The First
Epistle of Peter*, London, 1950. Catholic works: U. HOLZMEISTER, *Epistula
prima S. Petri* (*Cursus Scripturae Sacrae*), Paris, 1937; cf. also A. CHARUE
(*La Sainte Bible*, XII), Paris, 1945; P. DE AMBROGGI (*La Sacra Bibbia 2*, ed.
S. GAROFALO, Turin-Rome, 1949); J. MICHL (*Regensburger NT*, 8,
1953).

Admittedly the thesis advanced by H. Preisker[1] and M.-E. Boismard,[2] which claims that this epistle contains a baptismal formulary of the early Church, will not carry conviction with everyone;[3] but the relationship which Boismard establishes between this epistle and other New Testament passages on baptism, and other *topoi* of the primitive baptismal liturgy, are still valid. F. L. Cross goes even further when he tries to see a paschal liturgy in it.[4] Even if this supposition could not be verified, it merits a re-examination of the way in which the early Church celebrated the 'Christian' Pasch[5]—especially since other traditional data of the New Testament come into the picture here : the accounts of the Last Supper,[6] the passage in 1 Cor. 5.6-8, the setting of John's Gospel, and many of its pericopes.[7] Similarly, the exhortations to constancy in suffering are set within a wider, traditional formulary on persecution.[8] Finally, a few isolated themes of 1 Peter deserve theological study : not only

---

[1] H. Windisch, (H. Preisker), *Die Katholischen Briefe 3* (*Handbuch zum Neuen Testament*, 15), Tubingen, 1951; appendix p. 156-162.

[2] M.-E. Boismard, *Une liturgie baptismale dans la Prima Petri*, RB, 63, 1956, 182-208; 64, 1957, 161-183.

[3] E. Lohse, *Paränese und Kerygma im I Petrusbrief*, ZNW, 45, 1954, 68-89; C. F. Moule, *The Nature and Purpose of I Peter*, NTS, 3, 1956-1957, 1-11.

[4] F. L. Cross, *I Peter, A Paschal Liturgy*, London, 1954.

[5] Cf. H. Schürmann, *Die Anfänge christlicher Osterfeier*, in *Theologische Quartalschrift*, 131, 1951, 414-425.

[6] H. Schürmann, *Der Paschalmahlbericht* (Chapter IV, p. 63 n. 2); Id., *Der Abendmahlsbericht Lukas 22. 7-38 als Gottesdienstordnung, Gemeindeordnung, Lebensordnung*, Leipzig, 1955 (=3, 1960).

[7] Cf. H. Sahlin, *op. cit.*, (Chapter VI, p. 102 n. 5); G. Ziener, *Johannesevangeliun und urchristliche Passafeier*, BZ, 2, 1958, 263-274; cf. also A. Strobel, *Die Passa-Erwartung als urchristliches Problem in Lc. 17, 20f.*, ZNW, 49, 1958, 157-196. However, all these hypotheses are still very uncertain. For the relationship between Jn. 6 and the Jewish Pasch, cf. B. Gartner, *John 6 and the Jewish Passover* (*Coniect. Neot.*, XVII), Zurich-Copenhagen, 1959.

[8] W. Nauck, *Freude im Leiden. Zum Problem einer urchristlichen Verfolgungstradition*, ZNW, 46, 1955, 68-80.

the difficult *theologoumenon* of Christ's descent into Hell and his preaching to the 'spirits in prison' (1 Pet. 3.18-20),[1] but also the 'universal priesthood' (2.5-10),[2] the doctrine of good works,[3] the *Haustafeln* identical with those of Paul,[4] the idea of pilgrimage etc.

4. THE APOCALYPSE

In spite of its many points of contact with the Gospel and the epistles of John, the Apocalypse undoubtedly demands separate treatment (cf. Meinertz). The theological study of an apocalyptic work needs to be carried out on different lines from that of epistolary literature. The language of the prophet and the visionary, having thoroughly assimilated so many elements originally sprung from apocalyptic literature[5] while constantly

---

[1] B. REICKE, *The Disobedient Spirits and Christian Baptism*, London, 1946; J. JEREMIAS, *Zwischen Karfreitag und Ostern*, ZNW, 42, 1949, 194-201; W. BIEDER, *Die Vorstellung von der Höllenfahrt Jesu Christi*, Zurich, 1949; H. RIESENFELD, *La descente dans la mort*, in *Mélanges M. Goguel*, Neuchâtel-Paris, 1950, 207-217; R. BULTMANN, *Bekenntnis- und Liedfragmente im ersten Petrusbrief* (*Coniectanea neot.*, XI), Lund, 1947, 1-14; E. J. GOODSPEED, *Enoch in I Peter 3. 19*, JBL, 73, 1954, 91 f. For the Catholic viewpoint, cf. the commentaries; in addition, see J. CHAINE, art. *Descente du Christ aux enfers*, DBS, II, 395-431.

[2] J. BLINZLER, IEPATEYMA *Zur Exegese von I Petr 2. 5 und 9*, in *Episcopus, Studien über das Bischofsamt* (*Festschrift für M. Kard. Faulhaber*), Regensburg, 1949, 49-65.

[3] W. C. VAN UNNIK, *The Teaching of Good Works in I Peter*, NTS, 1, 1954-1955, 92-110.

[4] K. WEIDINGER, *Die Haustafeln. Ein Stück urchristlicher Paränese*, Leipzig, 1928; D. SCHROEDER, *Die Haustafeln des Neuen Testaments* (manuscript dissertation), Hamburg, 1959; cf. *Theol. Literaturzeitung*, 84, 1959, 549.

[5] K. L. SCHMIDT, *Die Bildersprache der Apokalypse*, in *Theologische Zeitschrift* (Bâle), 3, 1947, 161-177; H. LANGENBERG, *Die prophetische Bildsprache der Apokalypse*, Metzingen, 1952; J. CAMBIER, *Les images de l'Ancient Testament dans l'Apocalypse de saint Jean*, in *Nouvelle Revue Théol.* 77, 1955, 113-122; L. CERFAUX-J. CAMBIER, *L'Apocalypse de saint Jean lue aux chrétiens*, Paris, 1955.

evolving towards a very liturgical style,[1] conceals its theological contentundertheveilof signs and formulas, rather than expressing it in well constructed and logically developed passages. But nonetheless we are in fact dealing with a theology—stripped to its essentials, sometimes profound and often more apt for the expression of ideas than a systematic presentation would be; this applies, to take an example, to the relationship between creation (Apoc. 4) and consummation (Apoc. 21. 1-5). But its greatest strength lies in its theological vision of history as salvation-history, and in the relationship which it establishes between history and eschatology. It is this theology of history that has attracted most discussion;[2] genuine agreement on the fundamental import of temporal and eschatological history in the Apocalypse has however still not been reached. And judgement is made more difficult by the occurrence of several problems, among which the 'reign of a thousand years' (Apoc. 20. 1-6) holds special place.[3] Moreover, we must not neglect other themes of obvious theological interest, such as the picture of

[1] E. PETERSON, ΕΙΣ ΘΕΟΣ, *Epigraphische, formgeschichtliche und religionsgeschichtliche Untersuchungen* (*Forschungen zur Religion und Literatur des Alten und Neuen Testaments*, 41), Gottingen, 1926; J. COMBLIN, *La liturgie de la Nouvelle Jérusalem*, in *Ephemer. Theol. Lovan.*, 29, 1953, 5-40; G. DELLING, *Zum gottesdienstlichen Stil der Johannes-Apokalypse*, NT, 3, 1959, 107-137; T. F. TORRANCE, *Liturgie et Apocalypse*, in *Verbum Caro*, 11, 1957, 28-40.

[2] L. GOPPELT, *Heilsoffenbarung und Geschichte nach der Offenbarung des Johannes*, in *Theol. Literaturzeitung*, 77, 1952, 513-522; M. RISSI, *Zeit und Geschichte in der Offenbarung des Johannes* (*Abhandlungen zur Theologie des Alten und Neuen Testaments*, 22), Zurich, 1952; H. SCHLIER, *Zum Verständnis der Geschichte nach der Offenbarung Johannes*, in *Die Zeit der Kirche*, Freiburg in Br., 1956, 265-287; H. M. FERET, *L'Apocalypse de saint Jean. Vision chrétienne de l'histoire*, Paris, 1946 (German translation 1954); S. GIET, *L'Apocalypse et l'Histoire*, Paris, 1957.

[3] There is a bibliography in J. MICHL, art. *Chiliasmus*, in *Lexikon für Theologie und Kirche 2*, vol. 2, Freiburg in Br., 1958, 1058 f.; A. GELIN, art. *Millénarisme*, BBS, V, 1289-1294; H. BIETENHARD, *Das Tausendjährige Reich 2*, Zurich, 1955; R. SCHNACKENBURG, *Gottes Herrschaft*, 240-245.

Christ in the Apocalypse,[1] the way in which the Christian community 'understands itself' in face of persecution (Apoc. 12),[2] ideas on martyrdom, the conception of death,[3] and reflections on the celestial world[4] and angels.[5] The fact remains that the most important question, and the one which is again being urgently posed, concerns the meaning of history and eschatology.

[1] E. STAUFFER, *Christus und die Cäsaren*, Hamburg, 1948 (English translation 1955); K. G. RENGSTORF, *Die Anfänge der Auseinandersetzung zwischen Christusglaube und Asklepiosfrömmigkeit*, Munster-in-W., 1953; cf. also R. GUTZWILLER, *Herr der Herrscher, Christus in der Geheimen Offenbarung*, Einsiedeln, 1951 (a work of popularisation).

[2] For Apoc. 12, cf. A. KASSING, *op. cit.* (Chapter VI, p. 104 n. 2); the state of research is given in J. MICHL, *Die Deutung der apokalyptischen Frau in der Gegenwart*, BZ, 3, 1959, 301-310.

[3] Cf. E. GUNTHER, *Zeuge und Märtyrer*, ZNW, 47, 1956, 145-161; N. BROX, *Der Begriff 'Martys' im Neuen Testament* (a manuscript competition work), Munich, 1959.

[4] H. BIETENHARD, *Die himmlische Welt im Urchristentum und Spätjudentum*, Tubingen, 1951.

[5] J. MICHL, *Die Engelvorstellungen in der Apokalypse des hl. Johannes*, Part I, *Die Engel um Gott*, Munich, 1937; cf. (by the same author) *Die 24 Altesten in der Apokalypse des hl. Johannes*, Munich, 1938.

CHAPTER VIII

VARIOUS THEMES OF
NEW TESTAMENT THEOLOGY

MONOGRAPHS DEALING WITH LIMITED themes are to be welcomed, not only for particular reasons (such as a desire to follow an important theme all the way through the New Testament), but also for the more general reason of revealing the unity of New Testament theology (cf. Chapter I, section 3 above). We shall list the most important monographs, with an eye to the present state of bibliography in this field, and indicate some of the essential requirements.

I. NEW TESTAMENT CHRISTOLOGY

Christology is important, since in it the whole development of the early Church's message and theology is revealed, and the essential problems resolved : problems such as the relationship between the historical Jesus and the Christ of faith,[1] the transition of the first Palestinian community to Hellenistic Christianity, and the development of faith in the Jewish Messiah into a theology of the cosmic Christ. Contemporary essays still do not entirely measure up to what is required. Works which are

---

[1] Cf. F. RIGAUX's contribution to this series. (See p. xii above.)

already dated, such as A. E. J. Rawlinson's,[1] do not even take
sufficient notice of the new range of problems which in Bultmann's existentialist theology go to the heart of the basic questions of hermeneutics.[2] The book by the Dutch exegete G.
Sevenster[3] which traces the development of doctrine in each
group of writings in the New Testament and reveals their
christology is a substantial and, generally, a conservative work.
E. Schweizer's book is useful : his aim is to bring Christ close
to contemporary man existentially, by emphasizing the idea of
imitating Jesus in his abasement and glorification.[4] Without
forcing the texts and starting from the synoptic logia on the
imitation of Christ, Schweizer arrives methodically at the early
Church's formulas of confession : in this way, he manages to
construct a bridge between Judeo-Palestinian and Hellenistic
Christianity. Many questions are touched on here, even though
Schweizer has no intention of providing a complete christology,
and deliberately leaves Paul out of account; but he has discovered one of the main lines of New Testament christology,
and has revealed its permanent, ever relevant, significance. V.
Taylor's study, which is the culmination of two previous

[1] A. E. RAWLINSON, *The New Testament Doctrine of the Christ*, London-
New York, 1926 (=3, 1949). There is a good discussion of the theses
put forward by the history of religion school; in the same way, a treatment which starts from the religious hopes of the Jews and leads progressively right up to the latest stage of early Christianity is to be
preferred to a more systematic type of exposition.

[2] R. BULTMANN, *Zur Frage der Christologie*, in *Glauben und Verstehen*, I,
Tubingen, 1933, 85-113; *Die Christologie des Neuen Testaments*, art. cit.
245-267.

[3] G. SEVENSTER, *De Christologie van het N.T. 2*, Amsterdam, 1948;
cf. ID., *Religion im Geschichte und Gegenwart 3*, I, Tubingen, 1957, 1745-
1762.

[4] E. SCHWEIZER, *Erniedrigung und Erhöhung bei Jesus und seinen Nachfolgern (Abhandlungen zur Theologie des Alten und Neuen Testaments*, 28),
Zurich, 1955.

works,[1] strays less often from the beaten track; after an exegetical enquiry throughout the whole New Testament, Taylor tries to set New Testament christology down in a genetic and systematic way, and ends with a few suggestions for contemporary (Anglican) Christians.

The American, F. V. Filson, follows other paths : he studies various of the New Testament themes from a christological point of view—Christ and the Father, Christ and the Spirit, Christ and the Church, Christ and Christians.[2] O. Cullman has published a complete christology of the New Testament.[3] On the question of method, he declares himself in favour of a schematic presentation under the christological titles—reserving the liberty, in each case, of tracing the development of the title from Judaism to the end of the history of early Christianity. His work is a penetrating one : it is characterized by lucidity and the author's feeling for synthesis, and has a very wide following because of its essentially positive content. But it also reflects quite a few personal notions which are open to debate, and takes to extremes a supposition which in itself is valid : that, since the person of Christ cannot be separated from his work, and since his work is at root nothing but the revelation of the salvation of God, the only possible christology is a functional one, and any speculation on Christ's dual nature appears, in the light of the New Testament, as an absurdity.[4] In this way, he slams the door on the doctrinal development he had led us to hope for, and limits the horizons of New Testament

---

[1] V. TAYLOR, *The Person of Christ in New Testament Teaching*, London, 1958. The following works had already been published: *The Names of Jesus*, London, 1953; *The Life and Ministry of Jesus*, London, 1954.

[2] FLOYD V. FILSON, *Jesus Christ the Risen Lord*, New York-Nashville, 1956.

[3] O. CULLMANN, *op. cit.* (Chapter III, p. 52 n. 3).

[4] *Op. cit.*, 336.

christology in an unfortunate manner. Just the same, Cullmann's study will long remain, for the theologian, the most
stimulating of all, and we should like to possess a Catholic
exposition of the same breadth. At present, all that we have is a
number of limited studies (see below, on Paul and John); but,
any christology which aims at considering the basic problems
which we have indicated, and bringing them to a conclusion,
must cover the whole of the New Testament.

2. ECCLESIOLOGY

Since Christ's saving work is continued in the Church, ecclesiology is indissolubly linked to christology. Once again, the
problem can be seen in its true perspective only through an
examination of the whole New Testament. This sort of treatment has been attempted by N. A. Dahl on the theme 'the
people of God';[1] and all Scandinavian theology reveals a lively
interest in the study of the theme of the Church.[2] A. Oepke's
fine book on the new people of God[3] also embraces the whole
of the subject. The idea of the Church has always had a responsive audience among Anglicans.[4] Among German Protestants,
there are still many who think of a 'rift' between Jesus and the

---

[1] N. A. DAHL, op. cit. (Chapter II, p. 45 n. 2).

[2] G. AULEN and others, Ein Buch von der Kirche, Gottingen, 1951;
H. LINDROTH (ed.), En Bok om Kyrkans ämbete, Stockholm, 1951.

[3] A. OEPKE, Das neue Gottesvolk in Schrifttum, bildender Kunst und
Weltgestaltung, Gutersloh, 1950.

[4] R. N. FLEW, Jesus and His Church 2, London, 1943 (=1956); ID.
(ed.), The Nature of the Church, New York, 1952; W. F. HOWARD, The
Church in the New Testament, in Expository Times, 62, 1951, 207-210 (a
review of English books); L. G. CHAMPION, The Church of the New
Testament, London, 1951; L. S. THORNTON, op. cit. (Chapter V, p. 85 n. 6);
ID., Christ and the Church, London, 1956; C. T. CRAIG, The One Church
in the Light of the New Testament, New York-London, 1951-1953.

early community,[1] and yet F. M. Braun can justifiably speak of a 'new consensus' of opinion there.[2] R. Schnackenburg has tried to show that Jesus' message concerning the Kingdom of God was legitimately elevated into a community message concerning the Messiah Jesus who, in his condition of glorified Lord, now already exercises God's lordship over the Church and the world (D. Stanley: *Kingdom to Church*).[3]

But we still lack an exposition written on clear-cut ecclesiological grounds, which would deal with the early Church's *Selbstverständnis* as a messianic and eschatological community, and show us which themes and formulas this self-awareness used to express itself. In the field of ecclesiology, Paul must undoubtedly be allotted an exceptional role (cf. Chapter V above); but the other New Testament writings also contain many keystones which must be integrated into the complete building. We are becoming increasingly aware of the fact that our picture of the Church is incomplete without a description of its temporal condition and its external structure. J. L. Leuba's book,[4] which is concerned with this dual aspect— institutional and spiritual—is genuinely stimulating. The debate on the structure and the ministers of the Church—in which

---

[1] W. G. KÜMMEL, *Kirchenbegriff und Geschichtsbewusstsein in der Urgemeinde und bei Jesus* (*Symbolae Bibl. Upsal.*, 1), Uppsala, 1943; ID., *Jesus und die Anfänge der Kirche*, in *Studia Theologica*, 7, 1958, 1-27; H. CONZELMANN, *Gegenwart und Zukunft in der synoptischen Tradition*, in *Zeitschrift für Theologie und Kirche*, 54, 1957, 277-296; PH. VIELHAUER, *Gottesreich und Menschensohn in der Verkündigung Jesu*, in *Mélanges G. Dehn*, Neukirchen, 1957, 51-79.

[2] F.-M. BRAUN, *Aspects nouveaux du probleme de l'Église*, Fribourg (Switzerland), 1942 (German translation: *Neues Licht auf die Kirche*, Einsiedeln, 1946).

[3] *Op. cit.*, (Chapter II, p. 44 n. 4).

[4] J.-L. LEUBA, *L'Institution et l'Événement*, Neuchâtel-Paris, 1950 (German translation 1957). In addition, see (Catholic) V. WARNACH, art. *Kirche*, in *Bibeltheologisches Wörterbuch*, Graz, 1959, 432-459 (bibliog.).

important historical questions, as well as theological problems, are being touched upon—is now in full swing.[1]

3. THE SPIRITUAL CONDITION OF THE CHRISTIAN

Among the tasks belonging to New Testament theology, room must be made for a description of salvation as God realizes it in us through Jesus Christ : this will not be a study of justification alone (cf. Paul, Chapter V above), but a definition of the new life in this present age, confronted with the eschatological consummation—which is to say, existing in this state of tension 'between the times' and characterized both by the struggle against the ever-active powers of evil[2] and by that certainty of victory which comes to us from a salvation already achieved. On this point, the different authors of the New Testament each have their own distinctive vocabulary : Paul speaks of our

[1] Among a host of works, we should refer especially to: R. BOHREN, *Das Problem der Kirchenzucht im Neuen Testament*, Zollikon-Zurich, 1952; P.-H. MENOUD, *L'Église et les ministères selon le Nouveau Testament*, Neuchâtel-Paris, 1949; H. VON CAMPENHAUSEN, *Kirchliches Amt und geistliche Vollmacht in den ersten drei Jahrhunderten*, Tubingen, 1953; J. GEWIESS, *Die neutestamentlichen Grundlagen der Kirchlichen Hierarchie*, in *Zwischen Wissenschaft und Politik, Mélanges G. Schreiber*, Munster-in-W., 1953, 1-24; G. DIX, *Le ministère dans l'Église ancienne*, Neuchâtel-Paris, 1955; J. K. S. REID, *The biblical Doctrine of the Ministry*, Edinburgh, 1955; W. NAUCK, *Probleme des frühchristlichen Amtsverständnisses*, ZNW, 48, 1957, 200-220; J. COLSON, *L'Évêque dans les communautés primitives*, Paris, 1951; J. BROSCH, *Charismen und Amter in der Urkirche*, Bonn, 1951; J. COLSON, *Les fonctions ecclésiales aux deux premiers siècles*, Bruges-Paris, 1956; M. KAISER, *Die Einheit der Kirchengewalt nach dem Zeugnis des Neuen Testamentes und der Apostolischen Väter (Münchener Theol. Studien)*, Munich, 1957; E. SCHWEIZER, *Gemeinde und Gemeindeordnung im Neuen Testament*, Zurich, 1959.

[2] E. LANGTON, *Essentials of Demonology*, London, 1949; C. H. C. MACGREGOR, *Principalities and Powers: The Cosmic Background of Paul's Thought*, NTS, 1, 1954-1955, 17-28; G. B. CAIRD, *Principalities and Powers: A Study in Pauline Thought*, Oxford, 1956; H. SCHLIER, *Mächte und Gewalten im Neuen Testament*, Freiburg in Br. 1958; M. ZIEGLER, *Engel und Dämonen in der Bibel*, Zurich, 1958.

existence 'in Christ', John of everlasting life, and the author
of Hebrews of the anticipated possession of future goods (Heb.
6.4 ff.); the emphasis is laid, in turn, on the anticipation of the
full revelation of salvation (cf. Rom. 8.18-25),[1] on the possession of salvation here in the present (John), and on our condition as pilgrims (Heb.; 1 Pet.). This is a question of nothing
less than 'Christian existence' at the present time; to express this,
Bultmann, adopting an existentialist standpoint, has invented
the meaningful formula of 'eschatological existence beneath the
sign of faith'.[2] Today, it would be well worth elaborating the
data of the same kind concerning the Holy Spirit, grace and
the sacrament (without departing from the biblical categories). Even if such a work did not produce anything very
original where the content of the New Testament is concerned,
it would have the merit of bringing out the dynamic, *heilsgeschichtlich* and eschatological aspects of New Testament thought.
Even today, several attempts do exist along these lines in
the studies on the doctrine of the πνεῦμα and of the ζωή,
and on the conception of the sacraments in the New Testament
(see the relevant passages in this book); but these are always
limited in consequence to one particular field. A general treatment would reveal the organic link between Christ, the Spirit,
divine sonship (Gal. 4.6)[4] and the divine indwelling (Rom. 8.
9-11; Jn. 14.23), as well as the inward orientation of the sacraments towards ethics and eschatology; in short, we should be
better able to see what the riches and the 'tensions' of New
Testament soteriology mean for the Christian life.

---

[1] H. M. BIEDERMANN, *Die Erlösung der Schöpfung beim Apostel Paulus,*
Wurzburg, 1940.

[2] R. BULTMANN, *Theologie,* 266-348 (Paul); 421-439 (John).

[3] 'Life'.

[4] S. ZEDDA, *op. cit.* (Chapter V, p. 85 n. 2).

4. MORALITY AND ASCESIS

If we wish to realize to the full the ideal of the Christian vocation, we must also pay greater attention to New Testament
morality. Among Protestants, some remarkable studies on this
subject have appeared over the past years.[1] Especially among
the English and the Americans (people with a bent for the
practical life) do we note a marked interest in this field.[2] And
we cannot call this pure 'pragmatism'. Thus A. N. Wilder[3]
shows himself acutely sensitive to the theological problems
which Jesus' eschatological message raises for the moralist.
Catholic moralists are making increasing efforts to give a serious
biblical basis to their work. The favourable reception accorded
to F. Tillmann (who started out as an exegete), who tends to
base morality on the idea of imitating Christ, was entirely
justified.[4] Similarly, B. Häring[5] bases his morality solidly on the
Bible. For the rest, exegetes have not provided us with many
general expositions. Apart from works which deal with one
particular field (Paul, John), there is only R. Schnackenburg's
manual which outlines the whole moral message of the New
Testament[6] and a collective work by Belgian and French theolo-

---

[1] Cf. the bulletin on the state of research by H. H. SCHREY, *Rechtfertigung und Geschichte. Neuere Literatur zur Ethik*, in *Theologische
Rundschau*, 24, 1956-1957, 170-185; 199-238.

[2] L. DEWAR, *An Outline of New Testament Ethics*, London, 1949;
L. H. MARSHALL, *The Challenge of New Testament Ethics*, London, 1950;
A. N. WILDER, *Eschatology and Ethics in the Teaching of Jesus 2*, New York,
1950; C. F. H. HENRY, *Christian Personal Ethics*, Grand Rapids, 1957;
T. W. MANSON, *Ethics and the Gospel*, New York, 1961.

[3] *Op. cit.* (previous note); cf. also R. DUNKERLEY, *The Hope of Jesus.
A Study in Moral Eschatology*, London, 1953.

[4] F. TILLMANN, *Die Idee der Nachfolge Christi 4*, Dusseldorf, 1953; ID.,
Die Verwirklichung der Nachfolge Christi 4, Dusseldorf, 1950.

[5] B. HÄRING, *Das Gesetz Christi 3*, Freiburg in Br., 1956.

[6] R. SCHNACKENBURG, *Die sittliche Botschaft des Neuen Testamentes*
Paris, Munich, 1954.

gians which sets New Testament morality in the light of contemporary moral problems.[1] A great deal of work still needs to be done if we are to 'translate' into terms of Christian living the New Testament ethics and parenesis—which both depends on its period and transcends it so completely that it remains eternally valid. One final remark : in the search for a modern ascesis attuned to the needs of the laity, study of the New Testament can provide help which must inevitably prove decisive.

5. ESCHATOLOGY

We have already drawn attention more than once to the importance of eschatology in early Christianity, and to the diversity of attitudes and formulas that we find in this field. The study of the conception of time and history in the early Church must continue to hold the forefront of our interest[2]— along with the concern to bring out its attitude to the world and to history and, by doing this, to imbue ourselves with an eschatological vigilance; in short, we must remove the *eschata* from the marginal position which they hold (coming at the end of the symbols of faith) and make them the object of an urgent appeal to contemporary Christians. But this demands a

---

[1] *Morale chrétienne et requêtes contemporaines*, Tournai-Paris, 1954; C. SPICQ, *Vie morale et Trinité Sainte selon saint Paul* (*Lectio divina*, 19), 1959.

[2] Cf. Chapter IV, p. 57 ff., and the notes; on this point, cf. the fairly general treatment by T. PREISS, *The Vision of History in the New Testament*, in *On the Meaning of History*, Geneva, 1950; K. LÖWITH, *Weltgeschichte und Heilsgeschehen* (*Urban-Bücher*, 3), Zurich-Vienna, 1953; J. DANIELOU, *Essai sur le mystère de l'histoire*, Paris (German translation: *Vom Geheimnis der Geschichte*, Stuttgart, 1956); F. FLÜCKIGER, *Heilsgeschichte und Weltgeschichte*, in *Evangelische Theologie*, 18, 1958, 37-47; H. URS VON BALTHASAR, *Theologie der Geschichte 3*, Einsiedeln, 1959; K. G. STECK, *Die Idee der Heilsgeschichte* (*Theol. Studien*, 56), Zurich, 1959; R. SCHNACKENBURG, art. *Heilsgeschichte*, in *Lexikon für Theologie und Kirche 2*, vol. 4, 148-153 (bibliog.).

properly orientated 'existentialist' interpretation which, while recognizing that the eschatological event belongs to the future, would also emphasize its significance for contemporary man.[1]

Quite apart from this vast eschatological theology of history, the treatise on the Last Ends needs renewed attention. Even now a summary of the New Testament teaching, following the pattern of the one by H. A. Guy (Protestant),[2] could be of use. Particular questions, especially in the field of Pauline theology (see Chapter V, Section 7, above), have received more frequent attention. Here again, it would be interesting to show the unity of New Testament theology which exists beneath the diversity of formulas, and to bring the general theological view into focus. Protestant exegetes[3] are often tempted to give a novel, not to say highly subjective, interpretation to those apocalyptic conceptions of late Judaism which seem to be incompatible with our modern picture of the world. Catholic exegesis, on the contrary, defends the reality of the content of the promises which Jesus made concerning the future; but it must try to evaluate certain very symbolic images in a more theological way. For instance, the apocalyptic presentation of the last book of the New Testament which, like every literary genre, needs to be explained in accordance with the laws of its genre, and also in a manner responsive to the author's intentions, urgently

[1] Cf. E. Fuchs, *Hermeneutik*, Bad Canstatt, 1954; Id., *Zum hermeneutischen Problem in der Theologie. Die existentiale Interpretation*, Tubingen, 1959. (The author belongs to Bultmann's school).

[2] H. A. Guy, *The New Testament Doctrine of the 'Last Things'*, Oxford, 1948; cf. W. Strawson, *Jesus and the Future Life*, London, 1959; R. C. Smith, *The Bible Doctrine of the Hereafter*, London, 1958.

[3] In Germany: from the standpoint of existentialist theology: R. Bultmann, J. Kröner, H. Ott, E. Fuchs and others; from a different standpoint: E. Stauffer, *Agnostos Christos Joh. II. 24 und die Eschatologie des vierten Evangeliums*, in *In Honour of C. H. Dodd*, op. cit., 281-299; in England, *Realised Eschatology* (C. H. Dodd); cf. also T. F. Glasson, *The Second Advent 2*, London 1947; Id., *His Appearing and His Kingdom*. London, 1953; J. A. T. Robinson, *Jesus and His Coming*, London, 1957.

raises the question of the hermeneutic approach to evocations of the future. Unfortunately, this work has hardly begun[1] and it should preferably be centred on Jesus' teaching[2] which is very properly able to provide us with the key to later texts, and with the standard by which to interpret them[3]—texts, including the epistles (for example, 2 Pet. 3.10), which present us with pictures which can be very involved. Such a work would better enable us to set things in their right proportions. It is certain that we must emphasize the cosmic realization of salvation, and not individual eschatology : the deliverance brought us by God, and not his condemning judgement. But what Jesus has said on the subject will not allow us to dismiss this judgement altogether from mind[4] or to assert that the fate of the person immediately after death is of no importance.[5] Eschatology is a difficult topic for the exegete : it is a 'burning issue'. But it will also be a touchstone for New Testament theology, proving whether or not it can bring its tasks to a successful conclusion, whether it can manage to interact fruitfully with dogmatic theology, and whether it can bring the general body of theology the help it looks for in its task of confronting modern man with the call of the Word of God.

---

[1] Cf. K. RAHNER, art. *Eschatologie*, in *Lexikon für Theologie und Kirche 2*, vol. 3, Freiburg in Br., 1959, 1094-1098; H. URS VON BALTHASAR, *Eschatologie*, in *Fragen der Theologie heute*, Einsiedeln-Zurich-Cologne, 1957, 403-421.

[2] J. THEISSING, *Die Lehre Jesu von der ewigen Seligkeit*, Breslau, 1940.

[3] Cf. K. RAHNER, *Theologische Prinzipien der Hermeneutik eschatologischer Aussagen*, in *Zeitschrift für kath. Theologie*, 82, 1960, 137-158.

[4] W. MICHAELIS, *Versöhnung des Alls*, Gümlingen-Berne, 1950.

[5] But cf.: *La escatologia individual neotest.*, Madrid, 1956; A. FEUILLET, *La demeure céleste . . .* (Chapter V, p. 89 n. 2); P. HOFFMANN, *Der Christ zwischen Tod und Auferstehung nach der Auffassung Paulus* (manuscript dissertation), Munich, 1959.

INDEX OF AUTHORS